7 FIGURE COACH

How Start Your Own Coaching Business, Get New Customers, Stand Out from The Crowd, And Make More Money Today!

By

Patrick Ejeke

BONUS VIDEO WALK THROUGH

As I stated on the cover of this book,
you have **_won a huge bonus_**.
This a complete 9 video part series PLUS THE MIND MAP & THE CHEAT SHEET to boot. This is my way of saying thank you for buying the book.

Scan The QR-Code Below

PLEASE WRITE A REVIEW!

If this book helped you out in anyway, please help me to help others by writing a review!

https://www.amazon.com/dp/B08KJHCCS6

Still, if you did not get anything new from this book or you were not impacted in some way, I would still like to hear what you have to say. Either way, I will know what am doing right or wrong and to improve in the future. I wouldn't like to take your money and not deliver. So please, take just 2 minutes to let me know what you think.

Everyone is searching for help on how to improve their lives for the better and one thing they do look for are reviews. If this book has a lot amazing reviews with great comments, they will buy the book and read it and so the ripples effects of goodness spreads. But if it doesn't have any great reviews and comments, they don't buy the book and read it.

I know this book can positively impact and help someone and you can help that person by writing your thoughts and takeaways from the book.

Additionally, I would like to read your review and hear how this book has helped you in anyway at shape or form. My plan is to print every single review and hang them on my home office wall to read for inspiration and motivation throughout the day. Your great review helps me personally to stay focused and be able to validate all the hard work and lots of hours invested in preparing this book for you.

https://www.amazon.com/dp/B08KJHCCS6

Thank you again for reading this book and all of your support, I am truly honoured and grateful to have been of help. I look forward to helping you make this year the best ever for you and your family!

DISCLAIMER

The advice and strategies contained herein may not be suitable for everyone nor in every situation. This work is sold with the understanding that the Author and Publisher are not engaged in rendering legal, accounting, or other professional services. Neither the author nor the publisher shall be liable for damages arising here from. The fact that an organization or website is referred to in this work as a citation or a potential source of further information does not mean that the Author or Publisher endorses the information that the organization or website may provide or recommendations it may make. Further, readers should be aware that Internet Websites listed in this work may have changed or disappeared between when this work was written and when it is read.

Also, while we make every effort to ensure that we accurately represent all the products and services reviewed in this book and their potential for income, it should be noted that earnings and income statements made by me and others associated with the writing of this are estimates only of what we think you can possibly earn. There is no guarantee that you will make these levels of income and you accept the risk that the earnings and income statements differ by individual.

As with any business, your results may vary, and will be based on your individual capacity, business experience, expertise, and level of desire. There are no guarantees concerning the level of success you may experience. The testimonials and examples used are exceptional results, which do not apply to the average purchaser, and are not intended to represent or guarantee that anyone will achieve the same or similar results. Each individual's success depends on his or her background, dedication, desire and motivation.

There is no assurance that examples of past earnings can be duplicated in the future. We cannot guarantee your future results and/or success. There are some unknown risks in business and on the internet that we cannot foresee which could reduce results you experience. We are not responsible for your actions.

The use of our information, products and services should be based on your own due diligence and you agree that the author and anyone else associated with the writing and production of this book are not liable for any success or failure of your business that is directly or indirectly related to the purchase and use of our information, products and services reviewed or advertised in this book.

INTRODUCTION

Let's be clear about something here before we begin: everybody is an expert (or "expert enough") in at least one body of knowledge. It doesn't matter what it is.

Maybe you know how to sing a little bit better than everybody else, maybe you know your way around the basketball court, maybe have discovered a way of running a little bit faster, or maybe you know how to make money with Twitter or Facebook.

Regardless of who you're dealing with, everybody has at least one area of expertise. We can all agree on this because not all of us have the same experiences. Not all of us have had the same things happen to us.

It is precisely this difference in experience levels that make hanging out with our friends and family members so rich and rewarding. We get to look at the world from many different eyes and different perspectives. We also get to explore it through our shared stories at different times.

Since this is the case, did you know that people might actually pay for your expertise? This is the reason why the online coaching business is a large multimillion-dollar industry. People all over the world are interested in what other people have to teach them.

In fact, you only need to look at platforms like Udemy and the huge following of tutorial channels on YouTube to get a rough idea of the demand out there.

There is also a tremendous variety of **online education platforms** that help people improve their expertise in a wide range of knowledge areas. Online coaching is really just a variation of online education.

Of course, this is informal. You normally do not get some sort of certification or diploma after finishing a course. Still, the essence is still the same. People are looking for information that others possess.

What's more, people are willing to pay money to get this information. There is a tremendous demand for online coaching services because, let's face it, we live in a world that is increasingly expertise-based. How come? In one study conducted **by Metrix-Global LLC**, companies including Booz Allen Hamilton received an **average return of $7.90 for every $1 invested in executive coaching**.

Well, the internet actually has a paradoxical effect on people. As more and more information accumulates online, people feel isolated and alienated from any definitive claim of expertise. In other words, if you are going to claim to be an expert or a guru in a certain subject, you better know your stuff.

Most people lack that confidence, and that's why they hunger for specialized information. They know that, as information continues to grow on the internet, our knowledge becomes more and more specialized. It's as if we can only focus on topics that are an inch wide and a mile deep. We focus on the thing that we know and we rarely go beyond our comfort zone.

If we want to pick up certain information to at least get a practical understanding of it, that's when we need coaching. Because, let's face it, while you can figure this information out by going through all sorts of blogs and downloading all sorts of free resources, who has the time? Most people wish there more hours in the day because they're so busy.

Not surprisingly, there's a tremendous demand for online coaching because you cut straight to the chase. Instead of your client going through website after website trying to chase after the right information, you dish it out in such a way that they get all the information that they need, and they can acquire the knowledge that they're looking for on their own terms and on their own schedule.

Given these market realities, the demand for online coaching services will continue to rise in the foreseeable future. Platforms like Udemy, as well as free resources like Codecademy and YouTube "how to" channels, are just the beginning. This space is continuing to evolve.

Become part of that market evolution by starting your own online coaching business. This book gives you an overview of what's out there, the different models you can explore, and what to look for in terms of opportunities and potential problems.

But 1st, let's start with mindset.

The Right Mind-Set

First off, you have to have **the right mindset** to be a successful online coach. Without this you are doomed to failure. I will show you in this guide the mindset that you need and how you can develop it.

Online Coaching Plan

Having a plan for your online coaching business is very important. Without a plan you will never know if you are truly succeeding or not. I will show you exactly what you need to include in your plan so that you have the best chance of success.

Good People Skills

You need to make the right impression as an online coach and this starts with your **website**. There is no need to spend a lot of money on a fancy website. It just needs to be professional and we will explain what you need.

Know Your Audience

To make a healthy profit you need to attract the right clients. I have proven methods in this guide that will help you to find those clients. You will see that you have a number of options here. Some will require a small investment while others are free and will require effort on your part.

WAYS TO GROW YOUR ONLINE COACHING BUSINESS

There are a number of ways that you can grow your online coaching business and I have some good ideas for you in this guide. I also provide you with details of some useful tools that will help you to manage your online coaching business effectively.

With the advances in technology you now have a number of different ways to connect with people across the globe. People that are looking for coaches of all kinds can now find them very easily online. They have the freedom to find a coach that will really meet their needs who they will get on well with.

There are many people looking for online coaches that have the knowledge and experience to help them. If you specialize in a niche that is in demand, such as **digital marketing**, then if you follow the advice in this guide you will not find it difficult to get to quality clients. You need to keep them happy of course which we will discuss later.

Does Being an Online Coach Suit You?

Anybody can start an online coaching business today. That doesn't mean that it is a good fit for everybody. Do you have expertise in a particular niche? If so then you certainly qualify as an online coach.

There is no doubt that if you enjoy teaching others what you know then an online coaching business is a great way to do it. You can set your own schedule and work whenever you want to from anywhere in the world.

But you need to remember that you will always have to find new clients to make the whole thing profitable for you. There are different ways you can do this which we will cover in a later chapter. It is rare that finding a small number of clients will be enough to sustain a full-time online coaching business.

There are a number of **courses available online** that will teach you how to be a successful online coach. You can even obtain certificates from professional bodies to back up what you are doing. Online coaching is a great business to be in but you need to be prepared to provide the highest quality service to your clients and make a significant profit at the same time.

It helps you to Grow
When you decide to become an online coach, it will do a great deal for your own professional and personal growth. If you are an expert in your subject there is always more to learn and you will be committed to doing this so that you can provide your clients with the most up to date and useful information.

It is very satisfying to teach others what you know and to help them achieve their own goals. You will need to be a good communicator, and as you perform more coaching you will refine your communication skills. Dealing with all different kinds of people will open your mind and help you to develop as a person.

To be a good online coach you need to be disciplined and organized. If you commit to a coaching session with a client at a specific time then you have to be on time. You should **plan out your coaching sessions** to ensure that your clients get the best from them and feel like they have received a lot of value from you.

There is Good Money in Online Coaching
Online coaches charge hundreds if not thousands of dollars for personal coaching. If you are coaching several different people at the same time then you can charge on a per person basis which will bring you in a good amount of money.

Most people never turn what they know into hard cash. This is exactly what an online coach does. They are happy to provide their knowledge to others in return for a significant sum of money. **Ex-**

perts in the digital marketing niche can charge thousands for an hour of their time. The same goes for coaches in personal development and life coaching.

When you are starting out you will need to charge less than this but an hour of your time can still be worth hundreds of dollars. By providing personal one on one attention to individual clients they will appreciate this and will reward you handsomely for it. As long as you are providing good value people will be happy to pay you what you want.

Create your own Schedule
You decide when you will work. Obviously, you need to be around when your clients are and if they are in different countries then you need to plan for the differences in time zones. With today's technology you can send out reminders to your clients and use the Internet for all of your coaching sessions.

It is fairly easy for you to tell your clients when you are available for coaching. You need to be flexible here and make yourself available to your clients when it suits them. Some of them may have full time jobs and only be available at evenings and weekends. What you can definitely control is the number of coaching sessions that you provide in a day.

Very Easy to get started
You probably have all of the tools that you need to become an online coach right now. A laptop or desktop computer and an Internet connection and you are ready to go. Some online coaches claim that they can provide online sessions when they are on the move by using a tablet device. This is not something that I would recommend when you are starting out.

Clients will expect you to communicate with them using a messenger service such as Skype, Zoom, Facebook etc. You could offer your clients the choice of platform for your sessions. All of these services are free and you can even record the sessions that you have with your clients (there may be a small charge for this).

Everyone has email so you can use this as another communications medium. We recommend that you setup **Google Drive** or some other **cloud service** so that you can share materials with your clients. If you need them to see video footage then this will often be too large a file to send via email.

Then there is texting. You can send text messages anywhere in the world for very little these days. If your client likes this form of communication then ask them for their phone number and provide yours as well.

I recommend that you go for the best Internet package that you can for your coaching business. It is also a good idea to have a backup service as well. If your Internet access is down then you cannot provide coaching sessions. This is not going to go down well with your clients so always have a backup plan.

With high bandwidth Internet access, you can hold video calls and easily share your computer screen for demonstrations etc. Your clients will appreciate this as you are really helping them to learn what you know. Most people appreciate over the shoulder training.

THE BENEFITS OF SELLING YOUR EXPERTISE

Every person has at least some information or interest in information that they can potentially make money with. The next step is to figure out the forms this takes and what actual benefits you stand to gain.

Sell Information You're Passionate About
As I've mentioned earlier, people simply do not have the time to chase after information and then filter that material. They really cannot be bothered. Maybe they're too busy, maybe they feel that they do not have the proper expertise or the background to do it.

Whatever the case may be, they would rather go to somebody who is so passionate about a specific body of knowledge that they have put in the time, effort and focus in compiling this information from third party sources.

Think of it like going to a specialized librarian. If you're looking to, let's say, practice permaculture in a tropical setting, you can wrack your brains trying to go through all sorts of online libraries, chase down all sorts of arcane or obscure materials, or you can go to somebody who has an ebook or online course focused on that specific topic.

Get Paid to Talk About Stuff You are Curious About
Another benefit of selling your expertise is that you get paid to talk about information that you are curious about. This means that you have all the incentive in the world to feed your curiosity. When was the last time that happened at your day job? Chances are, there is a big disconnect between what you do for a living and the activities and subjects that you are personally passionate about.

When you sell your expertise in the form of a course, an online program, or some sort of book, you get paid to talk about stuff that makes you curious or which pushes you to investigate. This is actually one of the most fulfilling and gratifying benefits of selling your expertise.

You're not being paid to push a button. You're not being paid to do something that you've done millions of times before and which feels like it drains your soul. Instead, you are being paid to really pursue your passions.

Get Paid for Others to Pick Your Brain
One of the most fulfilling things people can do on this planet is to interact with each other where their understanding is not only challenged, but enhanced. Let me tell you, when it comes to hanging out with other people, one of the most satisfying and rewarding experiences you could get is when you get that "aha" moment.

When somebody shares something with you that you didn't know before, or shared information with you that enabled you to realize something that you did not know before, the sense of discovery and putting pieces together in your mind is a very positive experience. It excites a lot of people. And you get this opportunity when you get paid for other people to pick your brain.

They ask you question after question, and it's your job to basically take those questions and mentally pick them apart and come up with an answer. You are not only challenging your present knowledge, but you're also being paid to think.

Let's face it, not all of us are engaged at this level. Not all of us are getting paid to achieve that "aha" moment. You're basically getting money to develop as a human being. What's not to love?

Benefit from Passive Models of Selling Your Expertise
One of the key selling points of selling your expertise to others is the fact that you can develop a **passive income stream**. When you work for somebody else, generally speaking, you have to sell your time for money. That's the exchange. You agree to show up

at a certain time, at a certain place, to do certain things, and in exchange for that, you get paid. You trade your time for money.

This is a serious problem because, obviously, there's only one of you. You cannot be in two places at one time. Also, there are only 24 hours in a day. It's not like you have an infinite inventory of time to sell at any given day.

It is no surprise that a lot of people burn out from active income. That's what this is. When you trade your time for money, you are engaged in active income. If you stop taking action, you stop earning. Passive income works the other way. You work once or you work very little, and then the asset that you create continues to generate money.

The most obvious example of this involves books. You put in work to write a book. You write that book once, but once you have published it at Amazon Kindle and it continues to sell many times over, you earn many times from a book that you worked once to create.

In the brick and mortar world, a key example of a passive income is when you buy an apartment complex. You obviously have to work for the money to afford that complex, but once you bought it, every single month, your tenants have to come up with the rent. You just sit back and wait for the rent to come in.

From time to time, the property management company sends people out to make sure that the building is in good working order. But for the most part, you don't have to lift a finger to earn the rent money that comes in like clockwork every single month. That is the power of passive income.

The good news is, when you sell your expertise, the majority of these business models are passive in nature. You don't have to be there actively coaching people on a one to one basis. You can write a book, or you can shoot videos that people can view at their convenience. You can show up at a webinar and be recorded.

There are more passive versions of selling your expertise than active ones. You can stop selling your time for money.

Sell Your Personal Expert Brand

Wouldn't it be great if you earned more money the more you learned? Wouldn't it be awesome if you continue to grow your expertise in any kind of subject and end up getting paid more? That's precisely the position you put yourself in when you sell your expertise.

The more people buy your book, the stronger your brand becomes. The more seminars you give, the higher the likelihood that you will get interviewed or people would write about your seminars. In other words, the value of your business grows by you simply doing what you do and reaching out to interested audiences and building an organic following for your expert brand.

In other words, the more you sell your expertise, the more powerful your brand becomes. Compare this with working for somebody else.

Now, you may be the best employee on the planet and you may bring a lot of value to the table, but at the end of the day, only your boss sees your value and it's really up to that person whether they would promote you or not. It really boils down to their judgment call whether you're going to make more money or not. This is not the case when you're selling your expertise.

Because when you impress one person, it's not unusual for that person to tell another person. And then the people they know might be bloggers, so don't be surprised if there are all sorts of blog articles written about you.

Before you know it, people want to interview you and then your personal expert brand continues to grow every time you produce a product.

This is how experts build an author platform. They start out with books. They write down the things that they know in a particular specialized body of knowledge in the form of books. If enough of these books get publicized or if enough people buy these books and are impressed by your expertise, pretty soon they would want you to hold seminars or engage in one to one coaching.

You can shoot a series of videos and ask people to pay a one-time fee or a monthly membership fee to access those videos. You make passive income when you do this because you only work once to shoot these videos, but you make money every time somebody signs up to view those videos.

You obviously can make passive income every time somebody buys books that you have written in the past.

Similarly, your brand can get so big that you can hold a live webinar. Prospective audience members get notified that you are going to be holding an online seminar over webcam. They then fill out an appointment form and pay a fee. They show up, and you answer people's questions, and a recording is made so seminar attendees can have access to the seminar long after it's over.

Finally, as word gets out about your ability to help people and the value of the information you have shared, you can make quite a bit of money doing one to one coaching. You can do this on Google Hangouts or Skype, it doesn't really matter. What matters is people can pay you quite a bit of money on an hourly basis or even every fifteen minutes.

Depending on your field of specialty, you can command hundreds of dollars per coaching hour. This is not unheard of. People have done this before. In fact, top earners charge quite a bit of money for every fifteen-minute block of time they spend coaching people over the internet. This can get all lucrative, and it all boils down to developing a solid personal expert brand.

In the next chapter we will discuss the mindset you need to

become a successful online coach...

THE MINDSET YOU NEED TO BECOME A SUCCESSFUL ONLINE COACH

People often think that they need some special "insider knowledge" to become a successful and profitable online coach. This is not the case. What you do need is the right mindset to make a success out of online coaching.

You need to have the right plan and take the right action. Assuming that you are providing effective coaching sessions for your clients this is all that you need. If you were to analyze a successful online coach you would find that they have the following traits:

- **They are confident**
- **They have clarity**
- **They have a mentality of abundance**
- **They are always positive**

Basically, successful online coaches have a magnetic personality. People are easily drawn to them and look forward to their coaching sessions with them. Take a look at **Tony Robbins** for example. He has to be one of the most successful coaches of all time. So many people like him because of his magnetic personality. He started life as a janitor!

Unfortunately, there are a number of online coaches that do not succeed. This is because they do not have the right mindset for success. They do not exude confidence and as a result they take the wrong action. Clients are not confident in their ability to deliver what they need.

These coaches may be total experts in their niche. But this is not enough. If they do not have the right mindset to wow their clients then they are going to struggle. Successful online coaches never appear desperate for business (even if they are). They are always certain that they can get the right result for their clients.

The good news is that you can develop the right mindset to be a successful online coach. If you follow the advice in this chapter then you will be well on your way. So, let's take a look at the mindset changes that you need to make to be a profitable and in demand online coach:

1. You have to be Confident

People that hire you as their online coach expect you to be very confident in yourself and your abilities. They see you as their mentor and want to look up to you. If you don't have the right amount of confidence then you are going to struggle to find and keep profitable coaching clients.

You need to be confident in the way that you look and when you speak. One way to identify weaknesses in your coaching delivery is to record yourself providing a fake session. Use a video recorder so that you can play everything back and identify problem areas. Do this alone at first and then you can find people that will provide you with honest feedback.

Pay particular attention to the tone of your voice and your facial expressions. How do you greet your clients? If they ask you difficult questions how do you respond? How is your body language during a session? Do you look attentive and ready to listen?

2. You have to have Clarity

This starts with you being clear about what a successful online coaching business means to you. We all have different definitions of success so you need to define your own and work out how this will look and feel to you.

There is more to being a successful online coach than just money. Some people that have a lot of money are not happy with their lot in life. So, we recommend that you do not make money your sole focus with your online coaching business.

Think about how being a successful online coach means to

you emotionally and spiritually. Once you know this you can practice it all of the time. There are many online coaches out there that make good money but are not happy. This is not a place that you want to be in.

3. You need to think Solutions

Clients will come to you as an online coach because they are looking for solutions to their problems. You need to have the belief that you can provide a solution to any problem that your clients have. When you are first starting out you may be hit with some questions that you were not expecting so you need to handle this in the right way.

Unfortunately, if people are paying you hundreds of dollars for your time and expertise, they are going to expect you to have all of the answers right away. If you don't know the answer to something then you need to provide a credible response such as "there are several ways that you could approach this".

What you want to do here is buy some time so that you can come up with the right solution. When you first engage with your client, tell them that you are an expert and you are committed to finding the right solutions for them. Tell them that you may need to spend time after your call finding the most appropriate solution.

You can find yourself getting into a negative thinking spiral if you cannot provide the solution that a client is looking for right away. It is essential that you do not let this overwhelm you and always believe that you can find solutions for every problem.

4. Adopt the right Lifestyle Mindset

Because it is easy to get started as an online coach, a lot of people make the mistake of diving in head first and then end up working crazy long hours for very little money. We recommend that you come up with a lifestyle plan before you open your doors for business. There are limits to what you will do – working long hours for very little reward will soon grind you down.

Think about the return on investment (ROI) you want from your online coaching business. This is not just financial. You need to think about time freedom and satisfaction too. If you are a prisoner to your online coaching business then it is not going to last very long.

So, think about the money that you want to make and also the free time that you want from your new online coaching business. Also think about what will give you the most satisfaction from being in this business. This could be helping others for example.

Once you have your lifestyle plan worked out you can then decide how you will operate your online coaching business. You can choose what you will deliver to your clients and when so that it supports the life that you desire.

5. Be Goal Orientated

You need to set for yourself challenging goals if you want to be a successful online coach. Standing still is not an option – it may be easy for you to share your knowledge with the world but always be thinking about moving up to the next level.

Don't stay in your comfort zone or you will never realize your potential. You need to embrace change and different challenges. Think big and set big goals. If you get too comfortable then you can become complacent and your clients will notice this.

What other ways can you further your online coaching business? Can you turn what you know into a **successful digital product** that you can sell for a high price? Or what about a **membership website** where clients pay you each month to view training videos that you have made and learn from other resources?

6. Be a Collaborator

While it is possible to become a successful online coach on your own you are likely to achieve a lot more by collaborating with others. Having the support of a good network will have a significant impact on your ability to attract new clients and increase your income.

There are many different ways that you can collaborate with others. You can do a lot without having to travel anywhere. Find people that have authority blogs in your niche and work something out with them. Offer them a commission to advertise your coaching services. Write guest posts for their blog with a link back to your website.

You can also find influencers on social media that will promote your business. These people have large followings and can instantly connect with people that you could never find on your own. So have a collaboration mindset to really grow your online coaching business.

In the next chapter we will discuss the essential steps that you need to take to develop a successful online coaching business...

ONLINE COACHING PLAN

If you fail to plan you plan to fail. Have you heard that before? It is likely that you have heard it many times and the reason for this is because it is true. If you just jump in to your online coaching business it is not very likely to succeed.

In the last chapter we discussed how important it is to have the right mindset. So, we are going to put that into practice now by helping you to strategize your online coaching business. You need a plan and it needs to be good. Here are the essential steps that you need to take:

1. What do you really want?

There is no such thing as a perfect online coach. You can spend months on Google trying to find the perfect way to launch your new online coaching business and you will not find the right answer. This guide will certainly help you but you need to ask yourself some important questions before you get going.

There is no shortage of **online training courses** that will cost you a lot of money. Although the content in these courses is likely to be high quality you can never guarantee that it will be the right fit for you. As a starting point ask yourself:

- **What income do I want to earn each month?**
- **How many hours do I want to work on my online coaching business?**
- **What kind of contribution do I want to make in the world?**

Write down full answers to these questions because you are going to turn them into goals. The first is your income goal, the second is your lifestyle goal and the last one is your contribution goal. When you achieve all of these goals you will have an online coaching business that rewards you, provides you with the lifestyle you want and fulfils you.

2. Identify your Target Market

To succeed as an online coach, you need to serve your clients in a way that the market is not effectively doing so at the moment. You need to know who your target market is and what their pain points are and the problems that they have. It is important for you to align with their desires so that they are delighted to work with you.

When you are able to provide effective solutions to people you will become irresistible to them. They will happily pay you whatever you are asking. Providing the answer to their problems is what you need to be about so you need to know as much about your market as possible.

There are a number of ways that you can do this. You can look for conversations online to discover the problems that your target market is having. Your aim is to know more about your target market than they know themselves. Then just tell them that you have the answers that they are looking for.

Create a plan around this. Find out who your ideal clients are and find ways to identify the issues that they have. In a later chapter I will show you some great ways to find potential clients for your online coaching business.

3. You need to Stand Out

Until you are able to build a solid reputation as an online coach you need to stand out from the crowd. This is particularly important if you are going into a competitive market. There is nothing wrong with being in a competitive market – these tend to grow more than other markets do.

The best way to stand out from the crowd as an online coach is to deliver solutions that really make a difference to your clients. Make a commitment to develop an irresistible offer to them that solves one of their top pain points.

Use your creative mind here and offer the best way to fix their problems. This could be a series of one on one coaching sessions, a group coaching session for their employees, a series of training videos for company personnel and so on.

4. Price your Services right

Be committed to providing value to all of your coaching clients. When you have the solutions to their problems you are in a strong position and you can charge accordingly. Some people will try to knock you down on your price. We recommend that you avoid these people especially if they are "bargain hunters".

Never forget that the solutions that you provide can make a significant difference to your clients' lives. If your recommendations will save a business a lot of money then never be afraid to charge a high price for your expertise but also make that actually happens.

5. Take Action

Don't be a perfectionist. You do not need a website that costs a fortune and takes months to develop. Your website needs to look professional and explain clearly what you do. Anything more than that is just garnish.

Being resourceful is far more important than having a fancy website. Think about all of the people that you know and tell them that you are launching your new online coaching business. If they do not need your services then they may know others that do.

6. Setup a Support Network

Being an online coach can be a pretty lonely business. One of the best things that we recommend you do is to find a **good mentor or mentors**. There will be times when you are stuck on a problem for a client. With a good mentor in place it can be a lot easier to come up with the right solution.

Did you know that most good mentors have their own mentors too? Well they do and it is because nobody knows everything.

No matter how much of an expert you are in your niche there will always be something that you don't know or are unsure of.

Make sure that the people around you provide their support to you as well. The support of your spouse and your family is critical. It will also help you immensely if your close friends are supportive as well.

7. Scale your Online Coaching Business

Think of ways that you can scale up your online coaching business. Your focus here should be on providing you with more income and freeing up more of your time. Why not create **online training courses** where you will share your knowledge with others for a premium?

Another thing that you can do is to create an online community for your target market. Instead of them paying you for one on one sessions you can charge them a monthly membership fee to gain access to the community and its valuable resources.

In the next chapter we will discuss the best ways to deliver your online coaching...

GET TECHNICAL-ONLINE COACHING DELIVERY

The way that you deliver your online coaching to your clients does depend on your strategy. Some online coaches deliver to a number of people at the same time while others only offer one on one coaching. There are other online coaches that do both. Regardless of your approach there are common elements that you need to get right.

1. Prepare for your Coaching Sessions

It is essential that you are confident with your coaching sessions. If you are disorganized and just "wing it" then unless you are a master coach with bags of experience your delivery will not be perceived as confident to your clients.

Always bear in mind that your coaching clients are looking to you to provide answers to their questions. Your main objective must be as a solution provider that inspires your clients. When people are paying you top dollar for your advice, they expect you to be on the ball and give them what they want, so you better deliver.

With new clients ask them questions using email or through an online form to get a good understanding of what their problems and pain points are. Give yourself time to prepare for the coaching call so that you can research if necessary or speak with your mentors to come up with the best response.

There will be times when a client asks you a question that you can't answer. When this happens, you need to respond positively and tell them you need to look into the issue further to provide them with the best answer. You have to manage expectations here – your clients probably think that you have all of the answers already.

Prepare your first coaching session around what the client has told you about their problems. Using screen visuals is a good idea and will be well received so spend time getting these ready before your call. When you prepare everything beforehand it will give you the confidence to deliver the best possible coaching session.

2. Add Accountability to your Online Coaching

Your coaching clients are paying you for your advice and guidance so you need to have information prepared for them. It is also a good idea to create materials in coaching calls that provide a direct response to questions raised. Versatility is very important and it is not just about providing static materials.

When you are delivering your coaching sessions, focus on planting a seed. What you are doing here is providing ideas at the "seed" level that will take root with your clients and then start to grow.

Online coaching is a two-way street. The onus is on you to provide the solutions but you want the client to play their part as well. They need to take action against what you have discussed so introduce accountability into your sessions. Tell your client at the outset that they will need to be responsible for the agreed actions in your calls.

There are a number of good tools out there that will help you to provide this accountability. We will cover the best tools to use in a later chapter. Whatever tools you decide to use they need to be visible by both you and the client(s).

There are tools that offer a number of interactive elements such as **goal setting, calendars and journaling**. Use these to your advantage. It is essential that you keep track of the actions that you have agreed with your clients. This will include actions for you as well as actions for them.

What you want is a number of coaching sessions with a client for maximum profitability. It is pretty unlikely that you are going to solve all of their problems in one coaching session anyway, but when you have an accountability trail it will always prompt another session.

3. Be Flexible over Session Times and Platforms

If you live on the other side of the world to your client then you need to be flexible over times for coaching sessions. It is not ideal to perform coaching sessions in the middle of the night. But if that is the only time that your client has available then you need to make the sacrifice here.

We recommend that you have as many **conferencing tools and software** as possible at your disposal. A lot of people will be happy to use Skype and there are apps available for you to record your coaching sessions which you must do.

Always tell your clients upfront that you will be recording the calls. Explain that you will play the recording back afterwards to pick up on the agreed actions etc. Tell them that you do not want to write notes as this will deflect your attention away from listening to what they have to say. They should appreciate this.

You can offer a copy of the recorded coaching session to your clients if they want it. Another good reason for recording your coaching sessions is that you can learn from your mistakes. Take the time out to go through all of your early coaching sessions and think about ways that you can improve them.

4. Use Video Calling Where Possible

You want to create a strong connection with your coaching clients. One of the best ways to do that is to use video sessions so that they can see your face and you can see theirs. It is easier to pick up on visual clues during a coaching session than it is audible ones.

For example, if you are discussing a high-level concept you will easily be able to detect if your client is confused or is switching off while you are trying to explain something complex. You can straight away check with them to confirm that things are sinking in with them or not. It is never good for your client to leave a coaching session confused.

If you are coaching a group of people at the same time keep the numbers low (less than 6) so that you can monitor the reactions of the different clients. For group coaching you will need something more robust than Skype or the other messenger applications. You need to invest in a **video conferencing platform**.

Be sure to cover all your costs of using this type of platform in your pricing. Also make sure that you can record the sessions. If it is possible to record both video and audio then go for that option so that you can really assess your performance in the sessions.

5. Be Responsive outside of Coaching Sessions

None of your coaching clients are going to expect you to be available 24 hours a day. But they will expect you to respond promptly to any emails or other forms of communication that they initiate with you. Some online coaches choose specific times of day when they will respond to emails from clients.

While we are all for time management, we do not agree that it is a good idea to keep coaching clients waiting too long for a reply from you. We recommend that you respond to emails or text messages or any other form of communication from your clients as soon as possible. They will certainly appreciate that and will feel that you really care about them.

As an online coach your aim must always be to delight your clients. They are going to know people that you don't and if they are delighted with the service that you provide, they will happily tell others about it.

6. Be Empathetic

I mentioned that online coaching was a two-way street above and that the client has a responsibility to take action as well as you. If they are late delivering these actions then never try to ridicule them or get angry with them. You need to show empathy and explain to them that it is in their best interests to follow through with the agreed actions.

If a client wants to have a call with you late at night because they are struggling with something as a result of your coaching sessions, then unless it is completely inconvenient for you, I recommend that you have that call.

Listen to what they have to say and ask questions. If they need a bit more time to complete an action then tell them that is fine. This is not school and you are not a teacher who is going to place them in detention for not doing their homework!

In the next chapter we will look at **setting up a website** for your online coaching business…

SETTING UP A WEBSITE FOR YOUR ONLINE COACHING BUSINESS

Some people may tell you that you do not need a website to launch your online coaching business. We strongly disagree with that. The other thing that you may read is that you can use one of the free website platforms to setup a website at no cost. We disagree with that as well.

As an online coach you are going to be charging clients hundreds and later thousands of dollars for your coaching services. If you don't have a website then it looks like you are trying to do things on the cheap. When you have a free website it definitely confirms that you are a cheapskate!

You need your own domain name, web hosting and a professional looking website. There is no need for you to spend **thousands on some fancy design**. Your website needs to look clean and professional and that is all. It is not necessary to spend a great deal of time and money on it.

Some people are reluctant to have their own website because they do not know how to go about it. We will cover some of the basics here and there are plenty of good tutorials on YouTube which will provide the necessary details for you.

1. Choose a good Domain Name

Creating your coaching website starts with choosing an appropriate domain name. This is your unique address on the Internet. If your own name is unique name then you can use this as your domain name. If your name is John Smith or Mary Jones then this will not be an easy thing to do as the names will probably be taken.

You could go for JohnSmithCoaching.com or something like this. Or you could go niche specific with something like TheDigitalMarketingCoach.com. We have not checked that these names are available. You will need to check yourself using a domain registrar such as **godaddy.com or namecheap.com.**

As a general guide we would encourage you to go for a *.COM* domain extension if you can get one. They are the most popular by far and recognized by Google and all of the other search engines. If you can't get a *.COM* then look for a *.NET OR A .ORG*. You can also check out country specific domain extensions such as **.ca for Canada, .com. .au for Australia** and **.co.uk for the UK.**

Our advice is to make your domain name memorable and as short as you can. This is not always easy to do as most of the good names have gone. But with some trial and error you should be able to come up with a good name.

2. Web Hosting

You need web hosting to make your website live on the Internet. It is a place where you will store all of the necessary computer files to make your website operational and available for all to see.

There are many **web hosting companies** to choose from. They will usually offer different plans and prices per month. You need to budget between $10 and $20 a month for your web hosting. It is unlikely that your coaching website is going to get a lot of website traffic (visitors) certainly not at the start. You can always upgrade your hosting later.

Examples of good web hosting companies are **bluehost.com, hostgator.com and siteground.com**. Make sure that the web host you choose offers a one click WordPress install facility and has a large amount of disk space and bandwidth. You will also want to add an SSL certificate to your website for security and a lot of hosts now provide this free.

Once you have chosen your web host you will need to connect your domain name to your hosting. This is a bit technical and most web hosts will help you out with this. Alternatively, there are a lot of videos on YouTube that will explain how to do this. I also covered this in detail in blog post on **"How To Start A Blog For Free"**

3. Install WordPress

The next thing you need to do is to install the WordPress blog platform on your domain name. You can do this easily using one click software that most web hosts provide. Again, if you are in doubt ask your web host to guide you through this step or can find more information **on this post**.

WordPress is a content management system (CMS). It is very popular and millions of websites use the platform. It is totally free to install and use WordPress for your website. You do not need to know any web coding to add content to your new website when you use WordPress.

What you will need to do is to choose a theme for your new WordPress site. The theme is the web design element of your site. It is how it looks and feels and it is important to make a good choice here.

There are thousands of **free and premium WordPress themes** available. There are themes made especially for online coaching businesses. Go to your favorite search engine and enter "WordPress themes for online coaching business" and you will get some good results back.

You will need to log in to your WordPress installation and then you will see your dashboard. On the left-hand side there are many options available to you. One of those is to install a new theme. Select this and then upload the theme file that you downloaded. Activate it afterwards and your new theme is ready to go.

Another advantage of using the WordPress platform is that there are many plugins available to enhance your website. A good example here is a contact form where people can send you a message and this will be delivered to an email address of your choice.

There are plugins for other things too such as **search engine optimization (SEO),** special forms (these are great for asking your coaching clients to fill them out and let you know what their problems are), legal pages and much more.

A lot of plugins are free to use and some are available at a premium.

It is very easy to install plugins. Just log in to your dashboard and select the "add new plugin" option on the left-hand side. You can then upload the plugin file or search for a new plugin that you need. Install and then activate.

There are many good **tutorials on how to setup and use WordPres**s for your website on YouTube. This is not a technical guide so we will not include specific details here. WordPress really is the best platform to use for your new online coaching website so be prepared to spend a little time learning about it first.

4. Pages and Content

There are a number of important pages that you need to include with your new website and these are:

• **Home page** – this is the first page visitors will see when they type in your domain name

• **About page** – this is a very important page which tells visitors who you are and what you stand for

• **Services page(s)** – this can be one page or a number of different pages whichever suits your strategy. Here you will define the services that you provide

• **Contact page** – this is where a visitor to your website can contact you directly by typing a message and sending it to you.

• **Privacy and Terms and Conditions pages** – these are legal pages which explain how information that is provided by your visitors is managed. You can get plugins that will produce these pages for you automatically.

It is important here to make a distinction about pages and

posts. A page is usually static. Once you have created the pages above you will not need to change them very often. It is a good idea to test pages out to see how well they are converting for you and then make any necessary tweaks to them.

A post is information that is related to your niche and provides value to your visitors. We recommend that you make at least one new post a week about your niche. So, if you are a digital marketing coach for example you can write posts about:

- Social media marketing
- Search engine optimization (SEO)
- Email marketing
- Copywriting
- Driving website traffic

Obviously, you do not want to give everything away in your blog posts. Use them as a hook to get visitors to contact you about your online coaching services. You need to provide value in your posts but leave some questions unanswered so that your visitors will be able to learn more once they become a coaching client.

The reason that you want to create regular posts for your website is that it provides a reason for potential clients to come back and visit your site again. It is also good for SEO as the more unique content you publish the higher your rankings will be in the search engines.

5. Your Logo

We strongly recommend that you create a unique logo for your online coaching business. If you are not a graphic designer then there is no need to worry. There are plenty of talented people that can design you a great logo for a few dollars over at Fiverr.com.

If you want to do this yourself then you do not need to go out and spend a lot of money on graphic design programs like Adobe Photoshop. Just head over to Canva.com and you can choose a logo style and make changes to it to make it yours. This is completely free.

6. Email Opt In Form

Not many people are going to visit your website and become clients right away. A great way to stay in touch with potential clients is to create an incentive for them to provide you with their email address so that you can follow up with them afterwards.

You can create a special report for your visitors that tells them how to achieve something in your niche. It is best to address one or some of the problems that you have identified your target market has. So, for example if you are in the digital marketing space you could provide a report entitled "**5 Ways to Grow Your Social Media Presence**".

The trick here is to make the report enticing enough for the visitor to want to provide their email address to you. These days people are reluctant to give their email address as they know that they are going to receive promotional emails from you. So, make your free offer as compelling as you can.

You will need an autoresponder service to deliver emails to your email marketing list automatically. Two good services are Aweber.com and GetResponse.com. When you are starting out these will cost you around $20 a month.

You can set up a series of emails that will be delivered automatically to your new email subscribers with an autoresponder. Space these emails out over a few days as nobody likes to be bombarded with these messages. It is important to use enticing subject lines so that your emails will be opened.

It is also possible to send a broadcast email using an autoresponder service. Maybe you want to let your subscribers know that you have a special offer for them such as a 30-minute coaching session for free. You can choose who receives this broadcast. It can be all of your subscribers or just some of them.

You can easily create an email opt in form (where the visitor enters their email address) with autoresponder services. We recommend that you have a professional cover image created for your report and again there are many people on Fiverr.com that can do this for you for a few bucks.

7. Video

Another thing that we recommend is that you create a professional video of yourself describing what you can do for your clients. These days people would much rather watch a short video than read a lot of text.

It doesn't matter if you are not happy to appear on a video – just get over this and do it anyway. Coaching is a personal business and prospective clients will want to see your face and hear your voice before they make the decision to become a client.

You can host your video on platforms like YouTube.com, Vimeo.com and DailyMotion.com free of charge and embed the video on your web pages. These websites get a lot of visitors so you may get leads this way as well. Video is a must these days especially for online coaches so be sure to plan out a good video script and shoot a high-quality video.

If you need to pay someone to shoot the video and edit it for you then do that. It will be well worth the investment. Doing it yourself requires a high-quality camera, possibly some lighting equipment (which you may be able to hire) and video editing software to make your video the best it can be.

8. Social Proof

You need to get some testimonials for your online coaching business and add these to your website. If you are just starting out you can offer to provide some free coaching sessions in return for a testimonial.

Social proof is very important for all businesses and particularly important for online coaching. Potential customers will be looking for social proof that you do what you say and will offer them a totally professional service.

The best type of testimonial is video. When you offer your coaching services for free to get testimonials ask your client if they will be willing to appear in a short video. As a minimum you need a photo of the client and their business name and website address in your testimonials. This all adds to the authenticity.

Create the best Website that you can
When you have your own domain name and website it shows potential clients that you are serious about your business. This is good for your mindset as well. You are not embarking on a hobby here – this is a serious business that will generate income for you.

Having a good website makes you a lot more credible as an online coach. It showcases who you are and what you can do for your clients. You can add case studies to your website that explain how you have helped others in the past and the results that they achieved. This is great for your credibility.

Depending on the type of online coaching services that you offer, some clients will want to sign up and make payments using your website. This is especially true if you offer online training courses. It is less likely to happen if you offer one on one coaching but still possible so be sure to provide this option.

We recommend that you use your website as a lead generation tool. You either want prospective clients to contact you using your contact form or sign up to your email list by offering a great incentive.

Also use your website to deliver great value to your visitors. You need to establish yourself as an expert and authority in your niche, so provide them with great content such as blog posts to showcase what you know and what you can do. With valuable content on your site it will be much easier to convert visitors into leads and then clients.

Make it easy for visitors to share your content on social media platforms by providing buttons for the various networks that makes this easy. Make your website work for you 24/7 by adding a call to action on all of your pages and blog posts.

In the next chapter we will discuss how to get clients for your online coaching business…

HOW TO GET CLIENTS FOR YOUR ONLINE COACHING BUSINESS

You have identified your target market and now have your website setup and ready to go. It is time to get some clients for your online coaching business. We are going to show you ways to do this online. It is all about getting your message in front of the right people.

There are many tactics that you can use to get prospective clients to visit your website which will then convert them into clients. These include:

- Writing articles / guest posts
- Sending cold emails
- Running ads
- Creating videos
- Using social media
- Webinars

Social Media Groups

If you are targeting business customers then the best social platform to find them on will be LinkedIn. Some people have had good results using Facebook as well so don't dismiss this altogether. If your target market is individuals (e.g. you are coaching people to make money online) then Facebook is the best social platform.

The reason that LinkedIn and Facebook are so good is that they have groups of people that are interested in different niches. A search on either platform will reveal the groups that are available for a niche.

So, one of the first things that you can do is to join these groups and start posting some valuable content. People often ask questions in these groups or ask the group for help with a specific problem that they are having.

You can add useful posts to the groups as well. What you want to do is establish yourself as an expert in your niche as quickly as you can. People in the groups will definitely start to notice you when you are active and providing answers to questions and useful posts. A lot of coaches find clients using this method.

Pay Per Click (PPC) Ads
You can use Google or Bing to place pay per click (PPC) ads which are triggered by specific keywords. This can be a very effective way of driving targeted traffic to your website but you need to be careful with this as the costs can soon mount up.

If you like the idea of this method then the first thing you need to do is to conduct some keyword research. A keyword is the term that a user enters into a search engine when they are looking for something.

So, for example they may enter the keyword "digital marketing coach" or "internet marketing coach". Use the free Google Keyword Planner to find the most appropriate keywords (there are tutorials on YouTube for this). Create a keyword list then set up a campaign with Google Adwords or Bing Ads.

You will only pay when a visitor clicks on the ad and visits your website. Once they are on your website it needs to convert the visitor into a lead by them contacting you or subscribing to your email list.

Social Media Ads
Most social platforms now offer the ability to run ads to drive traffic to your website. Facebook and Instagram are really good at this and LinkedIn are getting better. These social media ads tend to be cheaper than Google Adwords PPC ads and you can specifically target people which you cannot do with PPC.

There are all kinds of analytics available for social media ads that will tell you how well your ad is doing. You can choose who to target and in which locations. Targeting members of niche related groups is a good place to start.

Write a Book

One way to really establish yourself as an expert in your field is to write a book. This will require time and effort on your part but it will be worth it when you have completed the book. You can get a professional cover made for your book and distribute it on Amazon Kindle and other platforms.

Some coaches create a hard copy of their book and give these out at networking events etc. A digital version is a good place to start. You can promote the book on your website as well and even give some free copies away to get you started.

Guest Posting

The idea here is that you write a high-quality article about your niche and then find blogs that are in the same niche and ask the owners if they will publish your post. Most blog owners are always on the lookout for high quality content to add to their blog. Some will even specifically offer guest posting.

You should be able to find related blogs that will accept your post. Some may charge you for the privilege, but if they get a lot of visitors then this can be a good deal for you. You need to add a link back to your website in the post that you publish so that the readers can find out more about you and what you offer.

Email Marketing

We talked about this in the last chapter. You will need to provide an attractive incentive for people to want to provide their email address to you and become a subscriber to your email list. Once they are on your list you can send them a series of emails, a few days apart, which provide value to them.

Email marketing is a very effective way to get coaching clients. But you must provide value in your emails. Of course, you can tell them about your coaching services in the emails but do not use a hard sell approach otherwise people will unsubscribe from your list.

Creating Videos

A lot of people do not like the idea of creating videos but they are a great way to drive targeted visitors to your website. YouTube is the second biggest website in the world and it gets a ton of visitors each day looking for all kinds of content.

You could create a series of videos showing how to achieve something that is relevant to your niche. These kinds of "how to" videos are always popular. Don't give too much away in the videos but make it very clear that you know what you are talking about. Be sure to mention your coaching services in each video.

You can set up your own channel on YouTube. Each video that you upload needs to be properly optimized with the right title, description and tags (all based on keywords) so that YouTube users can find your video when they search. Add a link to your website on the first line of the video description.

YouTube is not the only game in town. DailyMotion and Vimeo are popular video sites as well. They do not get anywhere near the traffic that YouTube does but they still get a lot of visitors. Make good videos and spread the word.

Webinars

A webinar is an online presentation where hundreds, if not thousands of people can all watch at the same time. You can find someone in your niche that has a large email list and do a deal with them. They will send out an email telling their subscribers about your webinar and you will provide the list owner with a commission on all sales that you make.

You will need to plan your webinar so that it is the best that you can make it. Your presentation should solve a problem that people have in the niche and provide value. You will give away some of your secrets and then if they want more, they will need to become a coaching client at a special discounted rate.

In the next chapter we will discuss the different types of online coaching services that you can provide to scale your business...

THE DIFFERENT TYPES OF ONLINE COACHING SERVICES

There are a number of different ways that you can sell your expertise as an online coach. We will look at the most popular ways to do this in this chapter. You can start with one method and then scale your business by using the other methods.

One to One Live Coaching

This is one of the most popular methods of online coaching. A client agrees to pay you for a single session or specific number of sessions. You then agree dates and times with the client to provide the coaching using a platform such as Skype or Zoom.

Once you are established you can charge very high prices for one to one coaching. Some of the top experts charge $10,000 for an hour of coaching. Less established coaches will charge a few hundred dollars. A lot of clients like the personal attention from one to one coaching so are willing to pay a premium for it.

The biggest disadvantage of one to one coaching is that you are selling your time. But it is certainly worth doing if you can sell a short amount of your time for hundreds or thousands of dollars.

One to Many Live Coaching

This type of online coaching is popular in the educational market. Professors will teach a small group of students at once and take questions from them. You can do this for your business as well but the logistics of getting all of the clients together on the same day and the same time can be tricky.

If you want to pursue this type of coaching then you can charge each person a specific amount that will total a bit more than you would charge for one to one coaching. It is tougher to run these sessions than it is with one to one coaching and again you are selling your time.

Training Courses

The problem with live coaching is that you are selling your time. Yes, you can make a lot of money with live coaching but another type of coaching that you can offer is training courses. A lot of people like to learn with online training courses. Websites like Udemy.com have grown significantly over the last few years.

It is going to take you quite a bit of time to create a high-quality training course. If you want to charge a lot of money for your training then you will have to create videos. Nobody is going to pay you hundreds of dollars for a few PDF documents.

The good thing about training courses is that you can create more than one. Look at the problems that people are experiencing in your niche and create a training course that provides solutions to all of these problems.

You can sell your training courses from your website or you can use external platforms to host your videos and documents. Remember that the external platforms will take a fee from you for hosting your courses. Usually this is a percentage of each sale so check all of this out before you go ahead.

Webinars and Membership Sites

With a webinar you will give away some of your advice for free and then provide more information in a high-ticket training course or through live coaching sessions. Webinars are more of a sales tool than a type of coaching but they work so well that we wanted to mention them again here.

You could create a membership site where people pay you a subscription each month to gain access to your live and recorded webinars. In these webinars you will provide the member with your most valuable information. You can also give your members other useful resources such as case studies, videos, documents etc.

In the next chapter we will look at the advantages and disadvantages of the different coaching models out there and the steps step guide on how to approach each one of them...

THE ADVANTAGES AND DISADVANTAGES OF DIFFERENT COACHING SERVICES SALES MODELS AND THE STEP BY STEP GUIDES ON HOW TO APPROACH THEM

Sell Your Expertise Through Live webinars

Live webinars

Live webinars involve actual live presentation in front of the camera. You're going to be talking about a very narrow range of topics. The seminar is very specific in terms of subject matter. What makes this different is that you're using a free-form approach. You just rehearse what you're going to talk about in terms of talking points, but everything else is up to the crowd.

People will show up and view you on their webcams. They then type in their questions and you'll answer these in real time. These live webinars are one-time events. However, you can set up an option where you can record the live webinar for viewing at a later date by people who have paid to view the original.

Appointments are set up for only one time. These can only be viewed when you're talking or people who couldn't show up can view the recorded version. That's it. This is supposed to be special. It's supposed to be a one-time thing.

Advantages

The big advantage here is you get to market anticipation for the seminar. This is supposed to be launched. It's a one-time thing and it's a special event. You have these things going for you. Also, when people sign up for your live webinar, it's a golden opportunity for you to sign them up to your mailing list. The form usually has an email collection component. You can use this to get more mailing list members.

The biggest draw to live webinars is the live interaction. You're actually coaching live. You're coaching a group of people at once. You cater to each specific audience's needs. These audiences vary so they all have different needs. This is why people get a lot more value from live webinars. They ask questions that are most important to them.

Have you ever gone to a live lecture and you get a chance to ask the lecturer questions? It's very interesting because different crowds have different questions. This adds to the perceived value of the seminar.

Every single seminar is going to be different because there are different crowds there. You actually get to charge more money for a live audience because of the impromptu and the improvisational nature of the call and response and audience dynamics involved.

This is a golden opportunity to highlight your expertise. People can see that you really know your stuff because regardless of the questions they throw your way, you know how to answer them.

Disadvantages

You really have to know your stuff. This is the biggest disadvantage of live seminars. The worst thing that you can do is to say, "I don't know." You're going to destroy your coaching brand if you let that bomb drop. The way to save face is to say, "I will get back to you," or "I will find out." Never ever say, "I don't know."

Also, please understand that a lot of other experts are using the same live webinar format. This is not new. This is revolutionary. Please note that depending on your niche, there might actually be saturation.

It might seem like you're the 100th person offering a live seminar on your topic. This saturation can lead people to believe that your stuff is not really all that valuable. After all, if it's that unique, why is everybody and his dog offering it?

Finally, you have to be quick on your feet. As awesome as the call and response dynamic may be. It can also be very rough on your nerves. You have to know what you're talking about. You have to listen to questions very carefully, understand them very quickly, and answer them in such a way that builds up your expert status.

Step-by-step guide

Step #1

Pick a live seminar software platform

At the very least, this platform must have a billing and promotional component. It must also have an email collection component or it must tie into your current email collection system for your mailing list.

Step #2

Pick a date

It's really important to pick the right strategic date. You don't want to pick a date that is too close because people might have made other problems. You also don't want to pick a date that's so distant in the future that people can easily forget. There has to be enough urgency in the date. This is how you increase the likelihood that lots of people will book your live seminar.

Step #3

Practice prepared materials as well as possible stuff that might come up

You have to know your stuff. You can't look like a fool. You can't look like a deer stuck on headlights. It doesn't really matter how much of an expert status you have managed to build up prior to this point.

All of that will go up in smoke if people think that you are a complete moron. Brush up on your expertise. As much as possible, prepare stuff and keep rehearsing until you have become completely comfortable with the materials that you're going to present.

Step #4

Look alive, motivated, and eager to help

If you're having a tough time trying to figure out the kind of persona you want to project, look at motivational speakers. Look at how they pump up the crowd. Now, I'm not saying that you should be the second coming of Tony Robins, but you have to look lively. You don't want to look like a stiff robot. That's not going to help improve your brand.

Step #5

Remember that your brand is on the line

Regardless of what you do, please understand that when you are in a live seminar, your brand is on the line. Things might get knocked loose. It might be an unforeseen accident. Any of these could be murder on your brands. Please conduct yourself professionally, don't insult people, be helpful, be positive, and be optimistic.

Step #6

Call people to action regarding your books

You have to understand that although you're getting paid for this live seminar, this should not be your only way to earn a living. You should also push your books, your password protected videos, as well as your live coaching services.

Finally, you should call people to action to share the word about your seminars. Tell people to tell their friends and family members about the stuff that they've learned and that you're always available. If people like your stuff, you'd be surprised how many people will refer you to people within their circle of influence.

SELL YOUR EXPERTISE THROUGH SCHEDULED WEBINARS

Scheduled webinars are simply pre-recorded video presentations that must be viewed on appointment. This is really a marketing trick. You should remember when people are made to feel that something is scarce and is going to go away soon, they are more likely to buy.

When you market your pre-recorded video as a webinar that people have to sign up for. People are more likely to sign up because they think that you have recorded it just for that event.

Little do they know that you've recorded it a while back to focus on one topic. People from all over the world can actually set an appointment to view it at different times. There's really no sense of urgency as far as you're concerned, but you create a sense of urgency on their end.

A distinguishing feature of scheduled webinars compared to live seminars is there is absolutely no question and answer section. After all, you're not in front of a live audience.

Advantages

As I've mentioned above, this is really a promotional trick. You build up hype for the "launch" of the webinar. This increases its perceived value. Once you have achieved this, you get a sneaky way to collect email addresses.

When people show up to sign up for the seminar, you can offer part of it for free. To get that benefit, they have to sign up to your email list. You then send an update letting them know that the seminar is on, they see the initial video, the like it, and they sign up for more seminars. This time, they have to pay.

The hype period where you are involved in the launch

enhances your author appeal. You're basically sending a psychological signal to your intended audience that you are worth waiting for and that your stuff is so valuable that they should wait for it.

Another advantage you get is that you get to use the launch date for your promotional outreach and marketing. Maybe you're buying ads. Maybe you're sending out emails. Maybe you're renting out other people's addresses.

Whatever the case may be, you can keep coming back to that launch date so there is a perceived scarcity for the webinar. Another advantage to this is the comprehensive value-packed nature of this specific type of video. This usually involves more preparation than long drawn-out video series. You are pushed to basically present your best materials in terms of graphic and content.

Also, the video that you are shooting is actually very short. You're basically going to have to compress everything that is awesome about a specific subject within a short time frame. This increases the likelihood that the video you come up with is exciting, engaging, and very personable. It will probably do a better job of building up your expert brand than the normal videos you produce.

Another key advantage that you get with this way of selling your expertise is the webinar platform that you use will take care of payment processing. In fact, some of these platforms even have promotional capabilities where people can refer their friends after they've signed up.

Since this is a coaching method where you pre-record, you stand to make passive exam. You record once and you get paid many times over because people sign up and view your materials many times over. The appointment system can be set to different dates.

This means that if people missed the launch date, they can

enter their email address and they can get a reminder to check out the next date the video will be available. It turns out that since the video is pre-recorded, it's available all the time, but you are pumping up the perceived value by only showing it at different times. People have to sign up for an appointment. To view the video, they have to pay for that appointment.

Disadvantages

The big drawback to this way of selling your coaching services online is the lack of engagement. Remember, this is canned content. This is not you talking or presenting live in front of a webcam. You have shot this material ahead of time and you're focusing on a fairly narrow topic.

This brings up the second disadvantage. You might actually be talking about stuff that isn't all that interesting to the viewer. This happens quite a bit. There's a recognized expert who's going to be holding a seminar on a specific topic.

When people show up to view the video about that specific topic, it turns out that the actual information that they're looking for regarding that topic is either glossed over, mentioned in passing, or not explored are. Talk about a let-down. You can bet that people are going to feel disappointed if they actually paid money to view the video.

Another disadvantage is that paid webinars carry huge pressure to deliver value "above and beyond" the normal value your books and canned video courses deliver. Otherwise, if people feel let down, your brand might suffer.

You might actually lose followers because they'd think that you rip people off or you over-promised and under-delivered. Please understand that since this is not live, you can't engage the call and response effect. This effect is crucial in making live interactions so much more meaningful and fun.

Step-by-step guide

To use this way of selling your coaching services, you need to do the following:

Step #1

Pick the right webinar platform

There's a wide range of platforms out there, but the right one for you should have payment processing capabilities (which means they should be able to take PayPal easily). It should also have promotional elements. When people sign up for a seminar, they should be able to invite their friends or share the materials on their Facebook wall. Also, the appointment setting system must be very robust. It must be clear as to when they're going to see the video and the system must remind them via email.

Step #2

Write your video script

Remember, you're not going to be sharing everything you know about your specific subject of expertise. Instead, you're going to focus on a fairly narrow range of topics within your expertise. Write your video script accordingly.

Step #3

Shoot your video

Don't try to shoot everything in one take. Try to get audio guides ready or some sort of visual aid. Also, make sure that there is enough helpful audio with the presentation. Now, please understand that this is not a slideshow. This is you speaking to the camera and trying to engage with the viewers using all sorts of props and graphical aids.

It can get quite rough. You might have to do several takes, but what's important is that the video comes off as smooth, authoritative, and professional as possible.

Step #4

Do outreach and promo

You have to promote. If people have signed up to your mailing list, send out an update. If people talk about your author brand on Facebook groups and Facebook pages, announce your webinar there. You might even have to buy Facebook page ads.

Step #5

Set up your appointment setting system

Make sure you set up the appointment setting system for your webinar platform. This way, when people respond to your ads, they can set up the appointment to view the video. Usually, you should ask for money at this point.

Step #6

Set up an email system to remind people

You should link the appointment setting system with the email system so that when people sign up, they automatically get a reminder that that they've already signed up and paid, and that the webinar is happening soon.

Step #7

Send out event notifications and gather emails

If you've done this right, when people set up an appointment, they've already signed up on your email list. However, if these are somehow disconnected, you can still get people to sign up to your mailing list. Of course, when people show up, they can then watch the video.

Now, how exactly can you make money off your mailing list? Well, once you have people on your list, you can notify them of another seminar you're having. You can also send them ads for affiliate programs. When people click on these affiliate links and they buy something, you get a commission.

You can also rent out your email ad blast to people looking for solo ads. They can pay you up to several hundred dollars per email blast. You can even sell your own products. Of course, you should push your own Kindle books as well as your courses on Udemy and other platforms.

SELL COACHING EXPERTISE THROUGH VIDEO COURSES

With this particular approach, you're going to record videos based on scripts that you have written ahead of time. Each script covers a specific topic. When the videos are viewed in totality, your viewers will get the important information that they wanted to learn.

You present these videos through a membership access area. In other words, these are not publicly available videos. You have to actually go to a specific website and use a login and password to access these videos. To get that login and password, your viewers have to pay a membership fee. You can charge them a one-time fee or a monthly recurring fee.

Advantages
The big advantage of selling video courses is that you get a passive income business. You only record the videos once, but you get paid that one-time membership fee, or every time somebody renews their membership. Whatever the case may be, you do the work once and get paid many times over.

Also, when you offer videos, they're more personable than books. Let's get one thing clear. It takes a lot of effort to read. You have to use your imagination, read between the lines, and exert effort to understand the information. That's a lot of work.

Video conveys a lot of information in a small space and in a short period of time. It is also very personable. When you look straight in the video, people can connect with your eyes. They can tell what your emotional range is based on the tone of your voice and your body language.

Another key advantage of selling video courses is you can get a lot of students if you use the right video course platform. Udemy is a very powerful and popular video coaching platform that covers most niches.

There are already thousands of people signed up to Udemy. If your course shows up in Udemy, there are certain preview sections as well as the servers' built-in search engine that people can use to find your course within the platform. By simply putting your stuff on Udemy, you can become visible to the students who already use that platform.

Disadvantages

The big disadvantage of video courses is that you might not cover the specific topics your viewers are interested in. It may well turn out that you covered 60% of the information they want to know, but what about the 40%?

Also, there's a risk that the information you talk about in your videos tend to be general in orientation.

Even though you're operating on an intermediate level of expertise or you're giving out intermediate level information, it still might be too general for your specific audience members. This might cut down on their interest or they might want to ask for a refund because you haven't exactly talked about what is most important to them.

Finally, if you're going to be selling video courses on a platform like Udemy, it may well turn out that there are too many competitors specializing in the same niche that you are in. This might also cut down on your sales.

Step-by-step guide

Step #1

Avoid competition as much as possible

Look for your niche on Udemy and see how many existing direct competitors you have. If there's too much for comfort, find a sub-niche with fewer competitors.

Step #2

Invest in better copywriting

Look at what your competitors are already doing on Udemy. How do they describe themselves? What kind of headlines and descriptions do they use? Come up with something better. Use clickbait-worthy titles and descriptions. Come up with a description that is worth sharing.

Now, if you don't have this skillset, you can hire veteran sales copywriters from places like Upwork or Fiverr to write these materials for you. Whatever the case may be, your stuff has to stand out compared to your competitors.

Step #3

Use Catchier Preview Videos

A lot of Udemy videos and other video-based platforms have allowed course providers to post a preview video. Don't waste this opportunity. Get a special video shot that really does a great job advertising the benefits people will get when they sign up for your video course.

Often times. When it comes to video course platforms, you really only have one bite of the apple. Don't waste it. Use a very catchy, slick, well-produced preview video so you can get your message across loud and clear.

Step #4

Over-deliver and Under-promise

You have to remember that Udemy is quite saturated. If you

are offering coaching in any subject area that has decent demand levels, don't be surprised if there are lots of people offering the same information. How do you stand out? How do you beat these people?

It's very simple: over-deliver and under-promise. When people sign up for your stuff, give them so much value that they can't help but write amazing reviews about you. Get them hyped about the value that you bring to the table that they can't help but get excited about the next course you're going to offer.

You can do this by simply promising more than your competitors, but delivering way more. In other words, you have to put your money where your mouth is.

Step #5

Use worksheets and other support materials that upsell your Kindle books

When people have signed up for your course, they will get support materials. Maybe these are worksheets or cheat sheets. Whatever the case may be, you should use these materials to upsell your kindle books so these should have links to your author profile.

You could also have links pointing to your scheduled Webinars. Finally, maybe you could have a link for people to sign up on your mailing list. Use your worksheets on Udemy or any other video course platform to build up your brand and get sales. At the very least, call people to action to share the word about your course.

Step #6

Create a course for all the sub-niches in your niche

For example, if your niche is wine making. You can start out by starting a video course on Udemy on how to make one type of wine. After that, you can focus on another sub-niche like sparkling wine. Make a video course on that. Then after that, use dry wines or something else.

By the time you're done, you should've covered all the sub-niches involved with wine. Do this regardless of the niche you are focused on. Maybe you're into animation, programming, or game design. Whatever the case may be, nail down the sub-niches by using the steps above.

This will ensure that you become a true expert within that niche. If a person is interested in that niche in whatever form, they will search for courses and if they see your name over and over again, they start to create an association between your name and a certain field of expertise.

SELL YOUR COACHING EXPERTISE THROUGH BOOKS

This method of selling your coaching expertise involves publishing books in a narrow range of niches. You're not going to publish a book that claims to talk about everything and anything related to your industry. That's not going to work.

The narrower your range of topics, the better. You get a much better opportunity to highlight your expertise. In your book, you address key questions involved in your niche. For example, you know how to brew beer at home. If you write a book on home brewing, you can talk about ideal conditions for brewing as well as common problems people encounter that prevent them from brewing amazing beer.

These questions are predictable. They don't come out of left field and it's very easy to control the flow and shape of the expert information and opinion that you're sharing in your book. The name of the game is to showcase your knowledge and build up your personal expert brand.

This book is really your business card. It tells the world that you know what you're talking about. People only need to read what you have to say on certain topics to be shown in no uncertain terms that you walk the talk.

Advantages of coaching through books

The primary advantage of this coaching channel is that it's completely passive. You work only once to compile or write the book. Maybe you had the book ghost written at Ozki.org or other low cost yet high value writing services.

Regardless of how you got the book made, you only do it once. The good news is that book can sell many times over in the course of a year. In fact, there are many book authors on Amazon Kindle who make tens of thousands of dollars off a book that they have written several years ago.

Remember, they only worked once to publish that book, but every single year, they're making all this money. You can do the same with books covering subjects within your expertise. As I mentioned earlier, when you publish a book, you stand out from the crowd.

You have to remember that in any place, there are likely to be experts in the same specialization as you.

However, not all of them can write a book. Maybe they don't have the time or the discipline to do it.

However, you have come up with a book and this gives you a tremendous competitive advantage. Each book must be set up properly for it to benefit you optimally. What am I talking about? Each book should promote your author website. If you don't have one, put one up because this is the website that highlights your expertise and expert status.

Every book you produce must have a link to that site. When they click it, they see your picture, your biography, your resume, your list of books and other experiences. In other words, they get the information they need to determine whether you are an expert or not.

The good news here is you can make quick work of developing a solid author brand in your area of expertise. How? You can write tons of books through outsource. You don't have to lift a finger to write this material. You just hire low cost, high volume, high quality writing services like Ozki.org. They would be able to drill down in your narrow expert niche.

They crank out book after book all bearing your name. The more books you publish, the bigger of an expert you become. Interestingly enough, the more books you publish, the less promotions you need to do. How come? Your older books have promoted your author website so much that when people join your author website's mailing list, you only need to send out an update telling people that your latest book has arrived for you to rack up quite a bit of sales.

In fact, a lot of expert coaches self-publish only using Kindle yet they make quite a bit of money and are recognized experts in their field. You can do the same.

Disadvantages

Please understand that just because you published a book doesn't automatically mean clients will show up. This is especially true if you're just starting out. If you're starting out from square one and nobody has heard of you, you're going to have to do promotions.

The good news is the more books you produce and the more you promote it, the easier it would be to drum up attention for your later books. Please understand that you're going to have to spend time, effort and yes, even money, to promote your books.

This is not one of those things that you build and all of a sudden, demand will show up. It doesn't work that way. You have to put in the time to drive awareness for your books.

Also, unless you publish in a grand scale, and I'm talking about releasing a huge number of books in a short period of time, your author profile can take a while to develop. Keep this in mind. This is not something that will happen overnight.

Step by step guide

Step 1: Focus on a niche

The first thing that you need to do to succeed in coaching through books is laser target niche focusing.

In other words, be clear as to what you want to specialize in and focus on that only. Master it. Seek out an area of expertise that is an inch wide, but plunge miles deep. Know it inside and out. This is how you build a solid foundation for your expert brand.

The flip side to this, which you also need to pay attention to, is that it has to be in a niche where there is enough demand. Let's be clear, you can be an expert basket weaver. But if nobody is really interested in getting coaching, much less books about basket weaving, you're not going to make any money.

Focus on a niche that people would actually pay money for. One way to estimate this is to go to Amazon Kindle and look at the sales rankings of books within a subject category. If you notice that a lot of the books sold that have lower rankings in the top seller lists have scores of sales scores of ten thousand or lower, you are in a high demand niche. This may be a good niche to select.

Step 2: Find your niche on Amazon Kindle

Now that you have a clear understanding of the niche that you want to specialize in, find your niche on Amazon Kindle. It has to be there and it has to have decent demand.

Step 3: Pick a sub niche that doesn't have much competition

Assuming that there is a lot of competition in your Amazon Kindle niche, feel free to dial down or skip down to a sub niche. The key here is to look for a sub niche that doesn't have much competition but still enjoys decent demand. This takes quite a bit of research. You can use tools like **Kdspy** to find keyword demand patterns on Amazon.

Step 4: Focus your book on your target sub niche

Now that you've identified the sub niche that you're going to specialize in, sit down and focus your book's fire power on that sub niche. Demonstrate through your book that you are an expert in that sub niche. Nail it down. Hammer it. Bring home the point.

Step 5: Create a link in your book that highlights your author brand

At the top of your book, you should put a link to your official author website. This official author website is not just your online calling card. It's not just a place to put a nice picture of you. Instead, it highlights why you should be considered an authority.

Maybe you should list down the books you publish there. Maybe you should list your awards and accomplishments. Whatever the case may be, it drives home the point that you are worth listening to if people are looking for information in the niches that you cover.

Step 6: Find related sub niches and write a book on that sub niche

Now that you have written your first book on a sub niche within your specific field of expertise, now is the time to write your second book. Find a related sub niche and write a book on that sub niche.

Step 7: Repeat until you have covered your whole niche

By this point, you have chopped up your field of expertise into different sub niches. You've also written a specific book for each of those sub niche. Keep repeating the process until you have covered your whole niche.

Step 8: Write more books to drill down your expertise and your niches

Within this niche, you already have one book covering sub niches. At this point, you should drill down.

What other topics within your sub niche haven't you talked about before? Write specific books on these. In other words, don't leave any stone unturned. Don't leave any issues unexplored.

Allow your author name to be found with all key words related to your niche. This is how you develop a niche focus that is an inch wide, but miles deep. Every mile down is a book and every quarter or 1/8 inch is a sub niche that you have a specific book on.

Eventually, when people find themselves on Amazon, looking through books related to your niche, they will always keep running into your author brand. It's only a matter of time until they click on the author profile and they end upon your author page where you list your credentials.

Regardless, thanks to this constant branding, chances are you will be recognized by your book's buyers as a real expert within your areas of expertise.

THE BEST PLATFORMS AND TOOLS TO USE FOR ONLINE COACHING

There are a number of useful platforms and tools that you can use in your online coaching business that will help you to stay on track and be the best you can be. These are particularly useful if you want to provide live coaching sessions.

You do not need these to start with. It is possible to provide a great one to one coaching service using Skype and the free recorder tool that converts your conversations into MP3 files. You can also use the free Google Calendar to keep track of your sessions. We recommend that you use these tools once you have a few clients.

Satori
This is essentially an all in one coaching client management system. With Satori you get a business intelligence tool and a customer relationship management (CRM) tool rolled into one. The interface is clean and intuitive.

With Satori you can market your coaching programs (and even build them), use it for the distribution of proposals and agreements, generate leads, collect payments and make online bookings and send out questionnaires prior to coaching sessions. Satori starts at $39 a month.

Coach Accountable
You get a lot of administrative tools to run your online coaching business with Coach Accountable. This includes the scheduling of coaching sessions, payment collection, sharing documents and the creation of individual coaching plans. You can get started with Coach Accountable from around $20 a month.

Nudge Coach
Nudge Coach is an online coaching platform that you can fully

customize. It will help you get clients and keep them and contains daily trackers that you can personalize for individual client requirements. You can also organize group coaching sessions with Nudge Coach and more. Prices start from around $25 a month.

Calendly

As the name suggests, this is a calendar application that will integrate with your existing calendar (Outlook, Google etc) allowing you to book sessions seamlessly. You can then send out booking links to your clients at dates and times you are available. This app makes you a lot more efficient with your session bookings. If you only run one calendar it's free.

Zoom

Zoom is a conferencing app used by a lot of online coaches. Your clients do not need to have a Zoom account to use the platform. All you need to do is setup a session and then send the join link to them via email.

You can record your sessions with Zoom and easily share recordings. There is also a webinar feature which works really well. Zoom integrates with most calendar apps and task management tools such as Slack. It's really good for coaching small groups. The "Business" plan is really good at around $20 a month.

In the final chapter we will look at the best practices for being a successful online coach…

BEST PRACTICES FOR BEING A SUCCESSFUL ONLINE COACH

Here are the 8 best practices that we strongly recommend that you follow to start your own profitable online coaching business. A lot of online coaches do not succeed but we believe that if you follow these best practices you will have the maximum chance of success.

1. Understand the Benefits

There are a number of benefits to starting an online coaching business. You can make very good money in online coaching and as your reputation strengthens you can charge even higher prices.

You have the flexibility to work from anywhere and work when it suits you. It is pretty easy to get started with online coaching and it will also help you to grow as an individual as you deal with more and more clients.

2. You need the right Mindset

You need to develop the right mindset to be a successful online coach. All successful online coaches are confident in what they do. They know what they want to achieve and are very goal orientated.

Successful online coaches are very positive in their outlook and they have an abundance mentality. Their magnetic personalities help them to attract clients to them. They also have a collaboration mindset and work with others to grow their business. They are solution providers and always think this way.

3. Plan your Online Coaching Business

You need to put an effective plan in place for your online coaching business and not just dive straight in. Start by be clear about what you really want by asking yourself what monthly income you want to generate, the hours that you want to work and the contribution that you will make.

Be sure to fully identify your target market and understand their pain points and problems. Create your plan around providing solutions to these problems. Find a way to stand out in the beginning, get your pricing right, create a support network and take consistent action against your plan.

4. Deliver Online Coaching Sessions Effectively

It is very important that you deliver your online coaching sessions in the most effective way. Avoid perfectionism here but be the best you can be. You must prepare well for your coaching sessions whatever type of coaching model you are using.

When you are providing live one to one or group coaching it is essential that you add accountability. Create all of the materials that you will give to your clients before the sessions. Agree actions on the session calls and document these for both parties.

Be flexible around your clients' needs when it comes to booking coaching sessions. Always conduct video coaching sessions where you can as it is important that you see your client and they see you. Be responsive to any emails or other communications your client sends you outside of coaching sessions.

5. Setup a Professional Website

We strongly recommend that you setup a professional looking website. Get your own domain name and web hosting and use the WordPress platform for your site. Choose an appropriate theme and create all of the necessary pages which add credibility. Have a professional logo made for your online coaching business and use this on your website.

Provide valuable content on your website in the form of blog posts and videos. Create an attractive incentive that you will give away in exchange for the visitor's email address so that you can follow up with them afterwards. Get testimonials for your online coaching services and add these to your website.

6. Getting Clients

Use a number of different strategies to find clients online. Look for Facebook or LinkedIn groups in your niche and become a member of these groups to provide value. Create PPC ads and test these for effectiveness on either Google, Bing or both.

Test social media ads on Facebook, Instagram or LinkedIn whichever fits with your target market. Check the analytics to see what is working and what isn't. Write a book around your niche to establish credibility. Write guest posts for high traffic blogs in the same niche. Create videos for targeted traffic and use webinars to sell your coaching services.

7. Different Coaching Services

There are a number of different online coaching services that you can offer to scale your business. One to one live coaching is very popular and you can charge high prices for this. You can also provide live coaching to a small group of clients.

You can create training courses for passive income. Video based training is best and you can charge the most for this. If you use a platform to sell your training courses they will charge a commission. Create a membership site where clients pay you each month to access valuable resources, weekly webinars and so on.

8. Online Coaching Tools

There are a number of useful tools available to you as your business grows. These are not necessary to start your online coaching business. Administrative platforms that help you to sell and organize your coaching sessions include Satori, Coach Accountable and Nudge Coach.

A good free calendar app is Calendly and this will integrate with your current Google calendar or Outlook. You can send out booking links directly from this app. Consider using the Zoom conferencing platform. This is excellent and you can record all of your sessions. Your clients do not have to have a Zoom account to use the platform.

We have worked hard to bring you this guide on creating a profitable online coaching business. The methods revealed in this guide are proven and will work for you if you apply them. Please do not just read this guide and do nothing. You are only going to create a profitable online coaching business if you take action.

In this guide you have everything that you need to launch and maintain a successful online coaching business. We have provided you with ideas on how you can grow your business as well and create passive income from it. Now it's over to you.

We wish you every success with your online coaching business!

PLEASE WRITE A REVIEW PLUS YOUR BONUS!

BONUS VIDEO WALK THROUGH

As I stated on the cover of this book,
you have **won a huge bonus**.
This a complete 9 video part series that PLUS THE
MIND MAP & THE CHEAT SHEET to boot. This is my
way of saying thank for buying the book.

To have access to these and many more, please send an email
to the address below with the subject line **"VIDEO SERIES"**
and I will send you details on how to access the videos.

admin@easyimreviews.com

PLEASE WRITE A REVIEW!

If this book helped you out in anyway, please
help me to help others by writing a review!

https://www.amazon.com/dp/B08KJHCCS6

Still, if you did not get anything new from this book
or you were not impacted in some way, I would still like
to hear what you have to say. Either way, I will know what
am doing right or wrong and to improve in the future. I
wouldn't like to take your money and not deliver. So please,
take just 2 minutes to let me know what you think.

Everyone is searching for help on how to improve their
lives for the better and one thing they do look for are reviews.
If this book has a lot amazing reviews with great comments,
they will buy the book and read it and so the ripples effects
of goodness spreads. But if it doesn't have any great reviews
and comments, they don't buy the book and read it.

I know this book can positively impact and help someone and you can help that person by writing your thoughts and takeaways from the book.

Additionally, I would like to read your review and hear how this book has helped you in anyway at shape or form. My plan is to print every single review and hang them on my home office wall to read for inspiration and motivation throughout the day. Your great review helps me personally to stay focused and be able to validate all the hard work and lots of hours invested in preparing this book for you.

https://www.amazon.com/dp/B08KJHCCS6

Thank you again for reading this book and all of your support, I am truly honoured and grateful to have been of help. I look forward to helping you make this year the best ever for you and your family!

OTHER BOOKS BY THE AUTHOR

Excerpts from My Book "How to Over Come Sales Objections In SEO"

Yes, granted you might not be in the SEO niche but the principles apply if you sell anything online.

Though this book is written with SEOs in mind, any business or company can use the principles and methods laid out here to achieve impressive results.

This is a book about how you as an SEO service provider (any business for that matter) can tackle problems that are associated with a sale.

But no matter what the product or who the other person is; the strategies discussed within this book will help you too. You don't have to be an SEO service provider to benefit from the principles and strategies laid out in this book. They are universal.

It's not about being a pro in business or being smart (though they all do help) but it's about your client. The other guy across the table or the guy on the other end of the phone. You will get to understand what stops a potential client from taking action on your services or products.

I will be breaking down the professional tips anyone and I mean anyone can deploy in their business. These will make you or your sales team skilled in closing sales. These are also the same methods that the most powerful sales companies and agencies use to close the toughest of sales.

So, am going to break this down into the following steps. 1st I will present general guidelines on overcoming objections, 2nd, I will move into common client objections followed by a Q&A section then 3rd, the summary of the whole process.

By the end of the book, you will have all you need to overcome the most common objections in SEO and close the sale. This, of course, opens you up to have better conversations with a potential client when you are in the middle of a pitch.

So, let's get down to it. But 1st, before we get into "how to overcome sales objections", let's talk a little about the "why" the reasons objections happen to start with.

Why Do Sales Objections Happen?

So, why do sales objections happen? Objections happen because a section or a portion of your sales process is weak. You didn't build enough rapport, you didn't ask them enough questions about them, you didn't give them a chance to talk – you talked for 45 minutes to an hour, and you didn't allow them to speak up. I mean, when you do a pitch, it's not a webinar; it's a pitch. And a pitch is only valuable if you're taking half of the time.

Behind every objection is a failure of a salesman to answer the burning question for every prospect, which is "What's in it for me?" SEO is an investment, what do they get in return? And if you don't have a good understanding, if you don't have a strong belief system that supports you, you won't know how to address the objection.

How you address an objection can be the tipping point for a prospect to buy your service or buy it from somebody else. However, with the right approach, you can easily win the conversation, turn that objection into an opportunity, and, ultimately, close that prospect.

Now that we are familiar with why sales objections happen, let's try and answer the question; does selling SEO need to be hard? Keep reading.

WHY SELLING SEO DOESN'T HAVE TO BE HARD

Okay, so selling SEO services isn't that hard, it's a lot easier than you think. As easy as any worthwhile endeavor can be. Most times, people's feelings that SEO is difficult is because of some deep-rooted misconceptions. Let's try and address them.

Misconception 1: I Need to Learn Everything about SEO

Think you need to learn everything about SEO to sell it?

The truth is you can start offering SEO services by understanding some of the core principles.

You should know enough to understand yourself how it works as well as accurately explain it to your client…but you don't need to be an expert at every facet of SEO to get started.

Knowing everything about SEO could result in you shooting yourself in the foot while in conversation with clients. There's no better way to create a glazed look in someone's eyes than talking about SEO in-depth.

Your job isn't to become an SEO expert: It's to translate SEO into a results-focused description that your client can understand.

That way, you can focus on painting the picture of how results through SEO will help their business. Doing that will help you close the deal.

Misconception 2: I Have to Do All the Work In-House

It's understandable to think that you might not have the time or ability to do the actual SEO work.

Here's the beautiful thing about offering these services: You don't have to do it yourself!

You can consistently deliver quality SEO work to your clients by enlisting the help of a white label SEO service, like The SEOResllers of which I am a partner.

In case the term "white labelling" or "reseller SEO" is unfamiliar to you, it refers to work done by another company on your behalf and sold under your name.

In addition to not having to perform SEO work yourself in-house, white labelling allows you to focus on providing great service to your clients by entrusting the work to professional SEO practitioners.

At SEOreseller, we have designed our services for scalability and we work with thousands of agencies around the world.

By using a scalable solution, you can offer SEO services to as many clients as you want without worrying about having to hire and train employees.

Time is your most precious commodity. To offer SEO services while holding on to as much time as you can, focus on managing the client and let us do the work!

Want some help getting started? Just GO HERE TO SIGN UP with us and we'll get you all set up!

Ok, now that we have the most common misconceptions out of the way, let's get into what SEO knowledge you need to start selling.

THE SALES PROCESS

Just to put things in perspective for you, overcoming objections is just 1 step in a series of steps that you need in every Sales Process. Of course, depending on who you ask, the Sales Process could be up to 8 steps or even 12 steps. For me, I prefer to keep things as simple as possible.

For example, Brian Tracy has a 7 step Sales Process. Steven Tulman of Social Pulse Marketing talked about a 10 step Sales Process in a piece he wrote for Status Magazine.

But the thing is, it doesn't matter how many steps you choose to adopt, there is always some form of objection on each step. Let me briefly run through the 7 Step Sales Process that I like to follow.

Step 1 Prospecting and Initial Contact

Before you start selling online, you have to know who you want to sell to. As simple as that may sound, but believe me when I say lots of people get that wrong including yours truly. When I was starting, I'll just put something up online without a clue who my customer or audience is. The biggest mistake to make.

The question is, how do you get to know them? Simple really. You have what could arguably be one of the greatest inventions of the 20th century, your mobile phone. Combine that with Google and the power of the internet and boom you are in business. Simply Google your customers. It can't get any simpler than that in the 1st step.

Then when you have found them, do the next natural thing, contact them. They won't sell your product to themselves. You have to put yourself in front of them and create that rapport that will carry you till you make the sale.

Get them to like you, trust you, be as close as you can to them without appearing creepy. No one will want to buy anything from you if you come across as creepy. Make them laugh...... Victor Borge said laughter is the shortest distance between 2 people. That gets you the best results trust me. It's difficult for some not to buy if you can make them feel good especially if they need what you have to sell.

After you build rapport, you qualify them. You try to figure out if your service is a match for their needs. Because if it's not, don't sell to them, right? There's only one reason you should be selling to someone, and that's because you can genuinely add value to their business, or their goals - you're able to help grow the business.

Step 2 Qualifying

The next in the process is qualifying them. This means; while you are gaining their trust and trying your hardest to make them laugh, you smoothly move into determining if they are a good match for your product or service.

Frankly, there is no need to push to sell someone something they don't need just so you can make a quick buck. What does that say about you and your business? That's the quickest way to sell yourself out of business. You just want to help them get what they want, value. That way they will be more than happy to give you their money in exchange.

The qualifying process involves you or your sales team asking Qualifying questions that are typically related to budget, authority, need and timeline.

Step 3 Needs Assessment

After the qualification is done, then you move to Needs Assessment. This is a process of asking follow up questions to understand the prospect. The goal is to thoroughly understand the prospect's situation, challenges, and motivations to potentially make a change by purchasing your product or service. There might be cases that the prospect doesn't quite know what they want or what will help the most in their business.

That's where your sales team will really earn their keep. You or your sales team need to listen more then you speak. Let the prospect empty themselves. It will also help them to anticipate any objects that the client might have.

Some example of questions that you might want to ask are-
What did you like or dislike about your previous provider?
What business problem are you hoping we'll be able to solve?

Describe your current situation.
Tell me how this situation will look when you've addressed your current business problem.

When all questions have been discussed, it is important that your reps verify their understanding of what the prospect told them. The best way for them to do this is by recapping what they heard and requesting confirmation. This ensures that the rep is on the same page as the prospect before proceeding to the next step. If needed, additional questions may be asked to clear up any areas the rep misinterpreted.

Step 4 Sales Pitch or Product Demo

In this sales stage, you can now tie the value of your product, service, or solution to your client's needs, challenges, and desired end state. To do this, you have to clearly communicate the corresponding features and benefits of your product offering.

You will agree with me this is a very good reason why you or your sales team should have a clear understanding of what is discussed during the need's assessment stage. This is critical if you hope to have a quality pitch and demo depending on what your products or services are.

Be sure that your reps make note of any specific benefits in which the prospect is most enthusiastic about. At the end of this stage, a proposal, if appropriate to your product or service, is typically scheduled for a mutually agreed upon date.

Step 5 Proposal and Handling Objections

You know, not all products and services require a separate proposal. Like I said above, depending on what you have, you might want to adapt it to suit your client's needs and aspirations. This should be done in such a way that all the information you have gathered so far since you started communicating with your client, are put into consideration and addressed properly.

It doesn't make much sense if the client has told you all their problems and you can't demonstrate a way that your services or products help solve them.

Try to focus or at the very least put a bit more emphasis on those areas that you discover are your prospect's biggest concern. It's at this stage that you experience objections and concerns which is the main topic of this book, how to overcome sales objections and land the sale of a lifetime. I will get to that soon enough, but just to close off the 7 steps in sales; here are the remaining two steps. It is just two more steps in what may be a very long sales cycle.

While this may seem to be one of the most important steps in the whole process, and in many ways, it is, but you won't get to this stage if you do not do a good job in all the previous 5 steps.

Step 6 The Close.

This is the point where your prospect commits to purchase or sign on to your product or service. Either they do this or they don't at this stage. There are hundreds of different closing techniques, tips, and tricks, but the most important thing to remember is that it is not a standalone event.

When the sale is made, prospects agree on your terms and price or negotiate for mutually beneficial ones. All objections have been addressed and all details are finalized for delivery, fulfilment, or related actions. This may also involve introductions to others in your company who will be handling these next steps.

Step 7 Following Up

This means exactly what it says, follow up with your client to make sure everything is good. This also may include, asking for more or expansion of the service you are already offering and as well as asking for referrals.

A great way to continue these relationships is through marketing communications such as updates about new offerings, industry news, an e-newsletter, or some sort of interactive rewards program. This way, your customers will always think of your company first when they have a related requirement or a friend who has one.

So, okay back to closing. As I said, you won't get to step 6 not to talk of step 7 if you don't carry out the 1st 5 steps properly and in order. Then and only then can you have a flawless close.

Now, the flawless close can't be done when objections happen, because most of the time there was a weakness at some point in your sales process. Either you didn't get them to laugh, you didn't get them to trust you, you didn't get them to like you at some point in the conversation. Or you didn't listen to them during the qualifying phase, or you may not have matched the right product to the right need. There are several reasons why, and we'll go through some of those reasons now.

So, we get into the main discussion of sales in SEO proper. Later on, I will be talking about some typical industry questions that you probably will likely encounter in the industry. They are classic questions and answers that lots of SEO service providers are asked all the time. One, in particular, is about the value of SEO.

You see, a lot of business owners know about their business and probably have and maintain a web presence. But they struggle to make the connection between their business and how SEO on their web property will translate into sales and profit.

COMMON OBJECTIONS

Pricing is one of the most common objections because there are lots of cheap services online. The issues are that many of the online services often stack up deliverables that don't bring significant results. You can rebut these statements by looking at the other offer and clearly explaining how much more value you will bring.

Another common objection is asking for a one-off or a trial. Here you can explain that Google wants to see consistency in your site becoming an authority as opposed to quick pops. Additionally, Google wants to see a holistic strategy including on Page optimization, links, and content.

But let me take them one after another and go drill deeper.

1- The Value of SEO

In discussing the value of SEO, when you talk to clients there are usually two scenarios. One is that they don't really get it. I mean how does what you do for them in terms of SEO translates into sales? Bear in mind that they don't see the results right away. Of course, SEO takes a while to kick in but even then, they won't really understand it unless you show them the starts and then walk them through how that is as a result of what you did a couple of weeks back. The second one is that you probably failed to listen to your prospect.

So, let's take them one after the other.

The 1st one-

Yes, sometimes your client won't get it so you have to educate them on that. Other times, it could be that you are not talking to the right person in the company or business. I mean the person whose job it is to make decisions within the company; you are basically talking to the gatekeeper. So, what you want to here is to be able to leverage some SEO stats - you have to know your stats off the bat.

So, later on in the book, I will be providing you with some pointers on what you should say in terms of stats. This shouldn't be a surprise. If you did a Google search, you will find that over 90% of sites on the internet are operated by small and medium-sized businesses. Out of this at least %91, you have about 80% to 90% of the folks behind these sites don't know much about SEO and it impacts their business.

So, that tells you that education is key here. And if you are going to do well as an SEO service provider, then you should make education a major focus in your business. It's not just your education, as the rules change often but also the education of your prospects.

Education is part of the game. You have a time frame within which you are meant to get that sale. You need to create desire, build excitement, and help your client see the value in the service that you are providing. You have to let them see just how much better their business will be doing and that it's capable of growing beyond what they can imagine.

So, SEO is an education game; you have to assume that everyone you talk to, it will be rare and few and far between that they will have knowledge that's equal to or better than yours. You will educate most of the people that you talk to about SEO.

And that leverages trust on your end. If you have enough SEO stats or digital marketing stats to throw out there, that just tells your client you know your industry and that you know what is going on right now.

The 2nd one-

It says you failed to listen to your prospect; this goes back to what I just mentioned earlier about you going through your sales process. Now remember it's not linear; you have to make sure that you build desire, you have to make sure that you offer value, and if you fail to do one of those, at your sales steps or your sales process, then you are probably missing out on the opportunity of closing the sale.

Now, as I told you before, I have made similar mistakes in the past. I have had a time where I have gone off the rails myself. I had this opportunity to pitch for an eCommerce site. But essentially, it became a pitch where they kept on talking about rankings and traffic, rankings and traffic, rankings and traffic… and repeatedly, the customer had said, what I want is s functioning site with traffic that wants to buy stuff.

Underneath all that, what he is really saying is "don't tell me about those technical mumbo-jumbos, just tell me if your skills can solve my problems and show me how". It's that simple.

And as soon as I gave him a yes, he said let's do it and he signed. How simpler can that get? I mean you have to be able to read your prospect in some way or form. Gauge his appetite for risk or his ability to stay with technical stuff.

Now, I'm not devaluing the technical portion of that conversation, because it did prove expertise, meaning he knew without a doubt that we were the pros and that we had their best intentions in mind, and that he saw our moral imperative. But there's only one thing that the business owner needed to hear: "Will doing SEO help me sell my products?"

That's it, that's all he needed to hear. Now, again, while we don't guarantee results, SEOs are experienced enough to make commitments. So, after we signed up to the SEO service, before their sixth month he is pulling in quite a good amount of traffic. But, it's also good to note that there are different kinds of traffic. Just because a site is pulling in tones of traffic that doesn't mean a thing if no one is buying whatever you want to sell. You need to be a bale to bring in buyer traffic. People who have their credit cards in hand and are ready to buy.

And this is an example of listening well to your customers; you have to ask them questions, they have to be talking half the time through the pitch because they don't want to hear "I'll rank you" and they don't want to hear "I'll get you a thousand visitors a day". They want to sell their products, that's the business goal. Your job as a salesman is to marry that business goal to what your service can deliver.

- **Pro Tips 1**

Below are just some of the stats that you need to pay attention to, and I think these are some of the most important stats for you to know.

- 93% of buying experiences begin on search. Not being present on search translates to lost opportunities for the client, so if you're ever thinking of just going for traditional marketing, think again.
- Can drive up to x22 ROI per dollar spent, and
- There are 60 billion websites online today (and growing); can you believe that? 60 billion websites.
- 91% of those aren't optimized. That's a sad story, but good news for SEOs out there.
- SEO is a 16-billion-dollar industry, so, you know, if I were you, l will be trying my best to get into the industry right now.

Now, let me just translate the opportunity for you. What that means is if only 10% of websites are optimized, SEO can easily be larger by a factor of 10. It could easily be a 160-billion-dollar industry; it's not a saturated industry, it's a very green field.

- **Pro Tip 2**

Translate the value of SEO into terms a decision-maker can understand. This is what I talked about earlier, about making sure that your client understands the value of SEO, and make sure that you don't overwhelm him with SEO jargon, just being able to show value to them is important. Having stats on top of your head or off the bat establishes trust signals.

Now, I'll move on to the next.

2- Pricing

This is a meaty conversation, and I had some, you know, not bad experiences, but challenging experiences on this one. So, I will be talking about pricing, and this is one of the most common objections I get, and you probably get as well from your clients. A lot of your partners would say, that the clients find the pricing expensive.

Or you might tell me, or tell your project managers, "I find your pricing expensive." And, if you're reading between the lines, the translation of this objection is "I do not see the value of what you just offered me, what you just pitched me."

That is exactly the problem. If you have a customer with a problem, an itch to be precise. He wants that itch scratched and you are not doing that. Then you are of no help or value to him. If a client says that your price is expensive then you haven't shown them that you can help them scratch the itch. If they know you can, the price will take second stage right away.

So, this goes back to the sales process of building desire or offering value to what you're providing. But really, our pricing isn't more expensive, and what I always like to tell the partners that I talk to is that we never claim that we're the cheapest.

That's one, and I always go into probing when I get these kinds of objections. I ask them, do you really get results for what you pay for? And, you know, you have to make sure that these clients are actually getting the right results, the right type of reporting, and we do provide that.

Working with my partners and sign up, we can offer your clients results, we offer you client dashboard logins, so your clients can access the google analytics dashboard in real-time and view the performance of your site and our SEO services.

We provide real-time reporting that comes at the of every cycle, we have the executive summary reports, and we have white papers and marketing guides.

So, I love this objection. This is the objection that is probably, for me the easiest one to overcome. Clients find the pricing expensive; so, my primary strategy really, is to tell people.

A} we're not the cheapest provider and
B} you get what you pay for.

Which really is the easiest thing to pitch off the top of your head. Now, let me give you a couple of reasons why this is easy.

You might not be aware, but it's actually normal, you can have end clients. You probably could have customers that come to you directly, especially locally. And despite facing the same objections that so many others face, you could be closing 8 out of 10 for every pitch. So, that will translate to an 80% close rate.

And you can overcome this because in order to make sure that you aren't cannibalizing potential profits with your partner agencies, (if you have those) you also have double or triple your prices locally. Now, why is it so easy to overcome?

First of all, I'll go back to sales. It's a belief system; I've seen how effective the service is, I've seen the businesses that it's grown, and I personally sincerely believe, that when we work on a campaign, they're going to get their money's worth, and I'm doing them a favor by closing to the best of my ability because they want to grow the same way that other successful businesses have grown.

So, by having a strong belief system in the service that you provide, you do not shy away from a pricing objection. So, I'll give you a great example though, when you cave to a pricing objection. Imagine that you take on a client who has been to another agency. (https://www.whitebasemedia.com/) And you take a look at their site and find that

2- **He was being charged say $300 for SEO**
3- **You find no optimization done on the site**
4- **non-existent or weak links from free blogs**
5- **a tone of blog comments (doesn't work today by the way)**

And the entire site is missing lots of the most important things that actually work today.

1- **No quality signals to Google,**
2- **No trust signals,**
3- **no well-crafted digital footprint,**
4- **No authority sculpting inside the website, nothing.**

5- No rich snippets inside the web page.

In his mind, this other SEO guy, he thinks he is saving money by only spending $300 at cost on his SEO. But in reality, he lost some of the relationships along the way; relationships he will never be able to get back.

And if for example, he has 11 other clients that he had onboarded, he personally spent out of pocket $300 for each of those accounts. What's 12 x $300? He was spending over $3,600 every month at cost, and he was burning relationships while doing that.

At the end of a year and a half, which is 18 months, he would have poured $64,800 down the drain. For nothing. Right? So really, you get what you pay for, and this is why I strongly advise that you need to be very selective with the partners you take in.

So, for any client, you take on you need to be careful and make sure you can deliver on any promise that you make. And why is that? You don't want to destroy relationships; you want repeat business and even better will be a referral and more business. Who doesn't like that?

And you have to have a great belief system about your service. Because the client doesn't know that you're good, and if you are not convinced of your expertise then you won't convince them either

- **Pro Tips 1**

No worries. So, on the pro tips, don't dance around the pricing objection, address it. I mean, sure you can dance while you talk to your client over the phone, but don't dance around the pricing objection, address it.

I'm not saying you have to affirm it, but you have to address it. Acknowledge the objection, then isolate the objection and act on it.

There are three golden rules in pricing, and I will talk about Primacy and Recency in a bit, but let me just go through the 1, 2, and 3 Golden Rules.

1- You never mention pricing first, and

2- You never let it stand alone. Lastly,
3- Never mention pricing last.

Having been on the internet and doing marketing, I have come to identify these 3 golden rules. These three golden rules will help you to overcome the pricing objection, or preventing it from becoming an objection.

Rule #1- is that you never mention pricing first; there is a phenomenon called Primacy. The first thing we hear tends to be stickier than everything else in the middle.

So how do you practice this? You don't go into a pitch, and start with "Hi, today I'm offering you a $2,000 package that will do this, this, this..." It doesn't work.

The moment you say $2,000, you might as well sing and dance and blah your way through the conversation. They will not hear anything past $2,000. So, you never mention it first.

Rule #2- Next, you never let it stand alone. So, you don't say, you don't go through the pitch, whether at the first or at the last, and tell them "And you get all this service, and look forward to these results, at the end of six months, all of that only for a six-month investment of $12,000."

What do you think? So, you never let it stand alone. You never let the pricing stand-alone. It's always... you always have to sandwich it between details. You will need to tell them, "The service plus this, this, this, and for that price, and for that investment, you get this, this, this, this." And you never mention it first, right?

Rule #3- Now, never mentioning pricing last. If there is anything more powerful than the concept of Primacy, it's the concept of Recency. And that is, the brain is biased to retain the last thing that was said.

This is so powerful, that whenever you call a help desk, or a credit card line, or whatnot, they'll tell you the brand first, so that they leverage Primacy, and they'll tell you their name last. So that you remember the name of the person you talked to.

The brain is biased to treat the last information or the last thing it heard to be the most important. When you say "And you get all of this for a six-month contract price of $12,000", everything you just said, you might as well erase. So that's the concept of Primacy, never letting it stand alone, and Recency.

- **Pro-tip 2**

If you don't work alone and you have partners that you attach yourself to, then it's important that you mark-up service by more than x1. I have to urge you, and actually, recommend that you mark-up services by x2 or even x2.5 retail cost when your portfolio is already built.

And actually, this next pro tip is a partner of a fellow SEO service provider. In the UAE because that's his market, he gives 30% on their first 90 days.

Right, so they've got a partner in the Middle East, and the strategy that he does to get people into contracts {because he does sell them contracts, not a prepaid subscription basis}, and his strategy is, he only doubles the pricing that they have on the dashboard during the first 90 days of the contract. And then, he proves that he can deliver results.

Now, in SEO the advantage is well, he is in a very ripe market, the Middle East is probably virginal to SEO - almost no one does it there, no matter how sophisticated and how advanced they already are.

So, almost any website he touches and implements On Page on almost overnight turns to gold. They're so convinced at the value that he's very successful at converting them from 3-month contracts to 6-month contracts. And by the time they cross the 3rd-month threshold, he puts them on regular pricing, which is the standard x3 of what my friend's services are.

And this is a good way to approach it strategically.

Excerpts from My Book "Virtual Real Estate Investing"

BRIEF HISTORY OF DOMAIN NAMES

As we know perfectly well, the arrival of the internet has been one of the greatest revolutions for humanity. This has changed the way of life for us all. Lifestyles change that includes, our interaction with one another, habits, and the way we do business. Every single aspect of our life has been impacted one way or another.

It's safe to say that work also has been impacted drastically. This has led to new opportunities and at the same time other professions obsolete.

The first domain was **www.symbolics.com** and it is therefore the oldest site in the world. The domain was purchased by the computer company Symbolics Inc, originally known as the Massachusetts-based Symbolics Computer Corporation, best known for making and distributing Personal Computers on a large scale.

In 2009, however, Aron Meystedt of XF.com, an investment company from Missouri, purchased the company and, therefore, also the domain.; the site is still active today and has become a sort of digital museum where users can retrace the infinite stages of the growth of the network from 1985 until today.

In addition to the www.symbolics.com website, 1985 saw the registration of only 5 other domains. A truly negligible number compared to the thousands of recordings that flood the various registrars around the world every day.

The millionth domain was registered as early as 1997.
As we can easily guess today, there are millions of domains scattered around on the internet.

Domain name syntax

A domain name is divided into two parts technically called labels, that are conventionally concatenated, and delimited by dots, such as example.com. That's according to Wikipedia. Such as- **example.com**.

The end of the "example.com" is referred to as Top-Level-Domain. "**.com**"

In 1985 there were only nine options to choose from: the first was **.com**, among others there were **.gov**, **.net**, **org**. And others like **.us**, **.uk** and **.il**, that is, the United States, England, and Israel, at the forefront. Although England has preferred to use a supra-domain before.UK, that is, co.uk, (where **.co** stands for commercial) but also, **.ltd.uk**, or **.gov.uk**. Other countries such as France, Germany, South Korea will come, together with others in 1986.

The birth of the internet is before 1985 and dates back to the 1960s. In those years, the USA developed a new defense and counter-espionage system. However, the invention of the domain name system (Domain Name System, DNS) gave the decisive push to the public to start using the network. It is a system used to assign names to hosts, or the "nodes" of the network within which the information is kept.

These names are useful for identifying the site the user is looking for. Without them, the search should take place through IP addresses, very complex numeric labels that uniquely identify network devices. The assignment of a name that is easily recognizable and memorable was, therefore, the key to facilitating the mass use of the greatest invention of the last century.

WHAT IS DOMAIN NAME INVESTING?

Domainers or Domain Investors, register domain names based on apparently generic phrases or words in the hope that these domain names may later be sold to businesses or end-users.

The purpose of a domainer is to buy the domains that he considers interesting, and that he can sell and make a profit from. If someone wants to develop a business linked to one of these domains, they will be ready to pay the price requested to obtain the right to use it.

In the United States, this is an old trade like the internet, and this kind of trade in domain names is highly developed and highly equipped.

Competition is very high. So, you need to choose domain names that you think you can resell and make a profit on.

The goal is to be the first to buy a domain that is not yet reserved, and which you think someone will need one day. Except that nothing says it will be exciting. So, buy sparingly, because you will keep your domains for months or even years.

The most representative domains are the domains linked to a generic activity (technology, decorations, games, fashion, etc.), as well as the brands of products that do not yet exist. But, since names in these areas have already been purchased, for the most part, you have little chance of finding the name that will be profitable.

The **domain trading business** is a tough one. It starts with small earnings, which you will improve over time. After at least 6 months, you should be able to earn something substantial. With the practice and the experience gained, you could over time turn it into a profitable business. And all this with only a few hours of daily work.

The domain trading is like investing in the stock market: you need to have a portfolio to limit risks and optimize earnings. Beginner domainers start with dozens of domains but begin to get serious from 50 domains. The professionals revolve around 150-300 domains.

Like any investment, domain names come with some risks. However, for diligent investors who consider risks and returns in-depth, domain names can become an investment that produces high returns.

MISTAKES TO AVOID WHEN SELLING YOUR DOMAIN NAME

Typossquatting-

If you want to go into domain trading, you must certainly be able to choose the right domain names but also avoid making some mistakes that newbies make when they are just starting.

The domain name that you will want to buy must be as original as possible and never a long word, but short enough to be easily remembered, these two assumptions are very important in this work and to create interest in buyers and increase the chances of success.

Forget the practice of registering domains with by practicing typossquatting. Typosquatting, also known as URL hijacking, is a form of cybersquatting (sitting on sites under someone else's brand or copyright) that targets Internet users who incorrectly type a website address into their web browser (e.g., "Gooogle.com" instead of "Google.com").

Apart from the fact that if you highjack a registered trademark; you run the risk of being sued but also it's kind of an expensive way to do **domain name trading** business. Besides, people who make mistakes when typing domain names are very few.

The two-letter reversal, the wrong domain extension, or a forgotten dash in the domain name is enough for a user to end up on the wrong website. The most popular websites are constantly attacked by typosquatters.

These speculate on the carelessness of users: when they enter a wrong URL they end up on websites containing advertisements, viruses, if not downright bogus pages, where you can be the victim of real scams or phishing attacks.

Typosquatters can end up in serious trouble with the law because, very often, registering a domain containing an error still violates the trademark right.

Since proceeding legally can prove to be a long and expensive process, it is always advisable to try to prevent this type of situation.

Many trademark owners use the strategy of simultaneously registering several possible domain variations with typos to protect themselves from competition or typosquatters. Website operators who use an easy-to-miss domain name should also consider logging variants with the most common errors. Once registered, domains with typos can be easily redirected via a redirect to your website.

To avoid Cybersquatting consists in registering or using a web domain in bad faith, to try to obtain an economic gain from registered trademarks and business.

Cybersquatters get most of their earnings by reselling these domains to those who own the rights to the exploited signatures.

Domain Discussion Forums

Forums on the web are sites where you can freely discuss topics that are focused on a particular niche. They have long been a part of the internet and the internet is home to thousands of them, and you can find them easily.

Many of them cover all kinds of topics where questions can be asked and answers found; others concern very specific topics such as "Domain Forums", where the main topic is domain names and all that concern a web domain. You can ask questions and wait for a plausible answer to your question or interact with other users by answering their questions.

Users and experts meet and discuss ideas, problems, or simply clarifications issues they might have.

Expiring Domains

When you decide to buy or sell a web domain, you are speaking improperly in the sense that buying or selling is not exactly the right words to use.

In reality, when we "buy" a web domain we are simply "renting" the use that you can generally decide for a year or 10. For the period in which you have rented it, it is as if it were yours and you can do whatever you want to do with it. You can decide to hold it or sell it if you want.

Being a rental and not a real purchase, the web domain in question will come to have an expiration date and you can decide whether to renew the use for a certain amount of time or leave it "free" knowing that someone else could re-rent it after you.

In the search for the best domain name, a completely wide ecosystem of business has emerged and it will keep evolving. This ecosystem is made up of expired domain sites to be auctioned. There are ingenious systems to beat the competition overtime when a domain is released, domain reservations expiring, advice on the value and potential of a domain, and much more.

Drop Catching Services and Back Ordering Services

"The domain dropcatch, also known as the domain backorder, is the mechanism that allows you to register a domain name once the registration has expired, immediately after the expiry."

To understand how it works we must also know the "life cycle" of the web domain.

During the "grace period", the domains can be renewed from the panel that is made available by the registrar to the customer.

When this period is reached the domain will not resolve the DNS servers and therefore will stop working.

If you renew your domain during this period, it will work normally after a few hours.

If you have not renewed the domain and the grace period has expired, the redemption phase will pass.

"The redemption period" is the period in which the domain cannot be renewed in the usual way, this is because the domain is not renewable and must be recovered. The cost of this recovery is higher than the usual renewal price.

To renew a domain that is in the Redemption Period, the renewal price is usually at least double the registration price (sometimes even much more)

If you have requested domain recovery, this procedure takes a few moments (after paying). Once it's active you have to wait a few hours.

If you decide not to recover it, the domain will go to the next state: "Pending Delete".

Upon reaching this state, the domain cannot be renewed because it is waiting to be removed from the registry. The next phase is that of "droptime", the domain can, therefore, be regained.

About forty-eight hours before the release, lists of domain names in droptime will be published on the main domain backorder platforms, so that customers and interested people can see them.

If there is a domain name in the list that interests you, you can try to book it through one of the backorder platforms.

If you don't want to use one of these platforms, you can try to register it manually after the droptime. The greater the interest in a domain, the less likely it is to be able to register it by hand.

TOOLS TO FIND NEW DOMAINS

Many websites on the internet allow you to "buy" a domain as there are other sites or tools that help us find new domains or better ideas regarding the name as a touch of originality never hurts.

"Namemesh" is a very interesting tool for discovering new ideas thanks to a wide range of customizations to be included in the name searches. There is a lot of information that you get just from the search results of this tool. Also, there is the possibility to decide which extensions to show with a simple click. Namemesh makes it easy to find good **SEO** friendly URL combinations.

If the keyword you were aiming for is already taken, you can try typing it in the "Lean Domain Search" search bar and you will have other suggestions that are close to what you want. For those who do not have enough ideas, for those seeking inspiration or for anyone wondering how to choose the right domain.

With "Bust a Name" an interesting solution is offered, just type two words, press enter and a large list of combinations and very interesting alternatives will appear. This helps you find original names. An excellent tool for the undecided, for bloggers who do not have clear ideas of what they want for a domain name. Or simply one who is looking for something new or simply to have a starting point on which to base themselves.

With "Instant domain search" just type a word and you will have a list of all the solutions, the free ones, and those already engaged. The Whois allows you to discover the owners and the suggestions' column gives you good advice for the alternatives in the domain choice.

Still "wordoid.com" and "Dot-o-motor" are two other valid alternatives.

DOMAIN APPRAISING SERVICES

Evaluating a domain or website is an estimate that takes into account numerous factors and can also be carried out with the help of online tools or expert advice.

Using domain brokers is perhaps the most reliable way to get an accurate estimate of the value of your domain.

There are also numerous online tools and software such as "Estibot.com" that allow you to estimate the value of a website or internet domain for free and immediately.

However, this software gives a very different and not very objective estimate, based on parameters which are not related to the US reference market.

Another alternative is the online forums that allow you to have a non-automatic but free web domain evaluation. Also, the evaluation is not done by robots but by individuals who have certainly gained experience in the sector.

Domain Aftermarket Auction House

The buying and selling of web domains through auctions is a constantly growing market. This is of interest both for those looking for a particular domain to associate with specific web activity and for those who want to build a new profession, exploring the opportunities of speculation that this sector can offer.

When you want to register a domain, the advice is to visit sites for domain auctions: **Afternic**, **SnapNAMES**, and **GoDaddy** are just some of the most famous.

Once the auction site has been chosen, it will be possible to (try to) register a domain or choose between expiring and auctioned domains. However, the actual value of the domain must be carefully evaluated: the domains with a high value are the short ones because they can be easily memorized, those containing keywords and those with a good "**SEO**". Websites such as "**Namebio**" allow you to collect sales information about a particular keyword and, consequently, to quantify the value of a domain containing that keyword.

After the necessary analyzes and after determining the available budget, it will be possible to make an offer for a domain or, when possible, to deal directly with the owner.

If, on the other hand, the goal is to sell a domain, after having evaluated it with the aforementioned tools, you can rely on sites such as "Escrow" to manage the transactions and the transfer of the domain itself.

Registrars

The registrar could be called "a broker".
Registrars have accredited companies that, in collaboration with the registry, deal with the sale and assignment of domain names, and manage them on behalf of their users.

Registrars also often offer other Internet-related services such as **hosting**, mailboxes, DNS management up to the creation of websites. After demonstrating that they possess the requirements, the registrars enter into a contract with the registry, to which they pay a monthly or annual fee, ensuring them certain guarantees in the management and resale of the domain names. Once the authorization to sell a domain name has been obtained, the registrar will choose independently not only the services to be offered, but also the costs for registration and any maintenance.

There are many on the web, sometimes impossible to choose one all with different prices and offers.

Certainly, some of the best known and most popular are: **NameCheap,**
Bluehost Domains, Google Domains, Register.com, Hostinger, HostGator, Domain.com.

DOMAIN MARKETPLACES

There are also several marketplaces dedicated to the sale of web domains, just as there are also marketplaces that sell everything and where domains can be sold. Websites focused on selling products where supply and demand meet.

There is an infinite number of them since the internet is now able to offer anything and, in every area, there is a lot of competition, so it is also for marketplaces.

The most famous, known and appreciated are certainly:
Buydomains.com- an excellent site worldwide that offers millions of domains for sale and which focuses mainly on "Premium" domains. By typing any keyword, all the related words will appear with the sale price, and you can also do an offer and negotiate with the price, an excellent site therefore also for those wishing to sell their web domain, and therefore looking for reliable customers, looking for the best.

Namecheap- One of the popular marketplaces. A marketplace is highly known and used by the most enterprising **internet marketers** who are looking for opportunities both in the sale and in the purchase. Through the search engine of the site, you can find the domain that most interests, and make an offer;

Domain.com- Another great alternative for our business.
This marketplace also offers different domain options, favoring "Premium" ones

Igloo- Another popular and beautiful site that offers domains in different markets, and of all types, including "Premium". It gives you all the necessary tools and information to meet your domain business needs. Igloo also offers several and beautiful custom templates that make it easier for you to negotiate online on the platform.

Fortunately, the internet today has made it possible for many to get involved and cave out a niche for themselves. Entering the business of selling web domains is one of the options that are available to anyone willing to put in the work.

Investing in websites is a process that allows any savvy user to make a sizable profit. The process should be three-fold: invest in flipping, parking, and developing websites. The better you can do at this, the more likely it is for your business to do very well, without a lot of long-term commitment.

Consider the different ways to invest in domain investing, or website investing.

1. **Invest in website flipping:**
   Here, you will purchase a domain name and start to develop the website. Once you have some level of secure footing, you then sell the website at a profit.

2. **Invest in domain name parking:**
   Here, the website owner registers a domain name. Then, with very little cost, they do nothing more than sit on it and try to sell it to those that may be interested in buying it.

3. **Invest in website development:**
   Purchase a domain name, work to establish the website,

and then hold on to it and profit from it.

In each of these situations, there is profit to be had. Domain name parking offers the lowest potential returns unless you have a very high demand for this type of domain name that a company feels they must have. Investing in a website and then flipping it is a great way to turn a profit, especially if you know how to set up a website fairly quickly and what it takes to get the **Internet marketing** going on it. Finally, owning and **developing a website** is the largest profit maker because the long-term benefits far outweigh the short term selling in either of the two prior options. Yet, the profits may be well off into the future.

Some **Internet marketers** use all of these methods and they do so very successfully. As your business grows, you too can make decisions later about how you use it. For example, you may find that you purchased a domain name and build a website you planned to own and run for some time. But, in a few months, the website is going strong and in turn, you have an offer to buy it that you simply could not refuse.

In all scenarios, the goal is to find and secure a website that will work for your goals. The development of that website hinges on the same factors as any other would.

You'll need to develop a website that offers good information, good keywords, and is an attractive domain name. Depending on the extent of your goals with that domain name, you'll want to build a successful website that people will want to own.

In this book, we'll take a look at what each of these areas can offer to you. We'll also talk about how to get started in each one. For many Internet marketers, even those that are just **starting**, these are the foundations of success in their business. This is how they make a sizable amount of money month after month.

DOMAIN NAME PARKING

The first and simplest form of making money from website investing is through domain name parking. Here, you can invest very little, usually just a few dollars. When you park a domain name, you simply secure the domain's use for another time's use. It can also be done to redirect traffic or for resale.

For example, perhaps you have come up with a fantastic website name and you wish to hold on to it before anyone else can snatch it from you. To do this, you simply purchase the domain name and it will sit there, usually with an "Under Construction" page up. The site may also be, "Coming Soon…" There is no deadline for developing the website. There is only the cost of renewing the domain name each year.

Those who determine they want to keep the domain name after the first year can renew it and start developing the website. This is a great way to finally get your website up and serving your purpose. You will then need to pay for hosting of the website at the point when you will develop it. This will include purchasing enough space for the site. At the time the website has hosting, it no longer is a parked website.

On the other hand, you may find it helpful to use it as a redirection page. For example, if you have a Yourname.com domain name, you may also want to purchase a Yourname.net domain name. Then, use the second page to direct traffic to the first page, in case people type in the wrong address into their navigation bar.

To make a profit selling a website, you may also want to consider domain parking. In this instance, you will park the website to simply hold on to the domain name. For instance, perhaps you have come up with a fantastic domain name you know a company may want at some point. You purchase it and park the website (meaning you don't even pay for website hosting for it.)

Then, you resell the domain name (at a sizable price, of course) and make a profit from it. It was very common for Internet marketers to do this type of transaction back in the early years of domain names, but it still holds today. Many businesses use this method as a method of increasing profits solely based on keywords and niche topics.

COMPARING IT TO REAL ESTATE

How does domain name parking make you money? Compare how it would work in a general real estate transaction.

With domain name parking, you are simply purchasing the land that someone may need at some point. For example, there may be a field out nowhere, in particular, that is open, filled with grass and rolling hills. Right now, it does not do much and doesn't have a lot of value. But, you notice it is just a few miles from a developing city. By purchasing it now, when the price is low for it, you can resell it later at a higher price simply because you were in the right place at the right time.

Domain name parking is quite similar. There is very little to invest in, just in purchasing the domain name. There is also very little to do with the website once you purchase it except hold on to it. Some Internet marketers will use it for Adsense, or other advertising, but unless the site does get a lot of traffic (especially if the traffic is not consistent) likely, it won't rack in too much money.

Turning A Profit

How can you turn a profit with domain name parking?

- Know who would want to purchase this domain name. Why would this name be a good choice down the road? Keywords, similarity to another, larger website, or some other reason?

- Determine if the domain name parking is the best recourse. Would it be better to further develop the website and then sell it? You'll find more on this in just a bit.

- Market the purchase of the domain name, alerting those who may be on your mailing list or otherwise involved in the niche that you have the domain name available. Many will consider it.

- Use keywords and a catchy phrase to attract interested parties. Think, what would someone in this niche be interested in?

- Hold on to it and watch the value grow. If you aren't in a rush, you may want to hold on to the domain name in a developing niche and sell it later when the value may be higher.

While domain name0 investing is a good option for many, it is not necessarily the only option. You should also be considering the other options you have with website investing, namely how you can make even more money from the purchase of it.

WEBSITE FLIPPING

Website flipping is the next step up in website investing. In this instance, you are moving one step forward: investing in a domain name, hosting the website, and getting the website up and running.

The best way to look at website flipping is to compare it to a real estate transaction: house flipping. With a home, you purchase the property at a low price. In this case, the website is virtually nothing. You may purchase a website already in place and improve it. Or, you can select a website domain name and start building from scratch.

The cost is again very small initially. Once you have the website under your control, you add to it, increasing its value just as a home investor would invest enough money to get the house in a higher-valued condition. They often modernize it, changing out any necessary appliances, and often repair the damage. By investing $20,000 to $30,000 into the home (not the website!) they wind up making a substantially larger return on their investment, perhaps even doubling the value of the property.

The same is true with website flipping. You come in with a very low price, build up the value of the website, and then sell it to someone (or a company) that can further carry it to success. The profit potential here is unlimited, depending on the niche and the overall success of the website you design.

Additionally, website flipping is not just about turning a small profit on getting a website started. It is also the process of finding underperforming websites, purchase the website, and increase the value of it. Then, you turn around and sell it for a larger profit. The fact is, many businesses online are still very new and they are often far less profitable than they could be.

To be successful at website flipping, you simply must know how to build a website with success. The more traffic it gets, the revenue it brings in overall high quality of the website will define if the website is worth more, and therefore if anyone will invest in it.

Advantages of Buying an Expired Website\Domain

There are some advantages to purchasing a website that already has been established, improving it, and then selling it off. For example, these websites already have an established audience. This means you do not have to develop an audience yourself. This could help you turn a real profit right away, simply by improving the search engine optimization of it or by installing an improved Adsense campaign, for example.

In addition to this, the website is likely already indexed in search engines. This is a fantastic tool because the website's ability to make a profit is likely to happen much faster. This can mean getting into the top search results faster. Even websites with very little attention likely have some type of backlink network already developed for it.

Another benefit of purchasing a website already developed is as simple as avoiding the Google Sandbox. This is only possible if you purchase a website that has made it through the first 12 months of life.

How To Buy A Website

Let's assume you will be purchasing a website that you want to **develop and flip**. It has already been in place for some time, and you know it is likely to be a great investment for your business. First off, you need to realize what the site can do for you and how it will fit in the strategy you are developing for your business.

You may wish to purchase a website that is already getting targeted traffic for the product or service that you are already promoting. By purchasing a website like this, you can then take all the traffic that is already going there and funnel it to your products and sales pages. For this to work well for your business, do be sure that the traffic coming to the website is high enough to warrant the purchase and quality enough to help turn a profit. High traffic does not mean you are getting good traffic. In the next section, we will talk more about purchasing a website and expanding and developing it.

On the other hand, you may just want to purchase the website and flip it. In this situation, you have to look for the right website to purchase. As a house flipper knows, it is more than just knowing what the actual problems are with the house. You also need to know the market for the house, or in this case, the website.

There is a risk in purchasing a website for the sole reason of flipping it. It can be very costly to make a mistake since you will likely be investing a good amount of money into the flip. In this situation, you need to ensure that you purchase websites that have the highest profit potential. You need to see a large result from the time and money you put into the site to make it worthwhile. On top of this, you also need to be sure that there is a market for purchasing it after you have created the final, finished copy.

Some of the best websites for this are underperforming **e-commerce websites** that are selling a product. The product they are selling should be in a well-established market. Look for a market that may be just starting to take off. In addition to this, be sure that the website itself has potential. For example, if it already has great search engine optimization, chances are good it may not get much better. Of course, the website's owners have to be willing to sell.

To make a profit from flipping websites, you have to master the following:

- Choose the proper website that can provide you with the likely potential sale you are hoping for.

- Implement changes quickly. This usually includes making a few changes to see a significant increase in the functioning and profitability of the website, in multiple areas.

- Get a double-digit increase in sales for the website, a sure sign the website is profitable.

- Get the work done and working for you before the general marketplace gets caught up to you.

- Do this and you can make a sizable profit on the website

by selling it for a premium.

- Don't wait so long that the Internet is saturated with those who are selling the product or service you are.

It is important to remember that the Internet is one of the fastest moving marketplaces anywhere. The competitiveness of the web is also just as fast-moving. To buy and flip websites with success, you will need to know what to do, how to do it, and get it done as soon as possible. You should also be up to date on the movement on the web, including the strategies helping the web to move fast.

Take into consideration this method of website investing carefully. It takes the combination of just the right scenario to make a profit. This method of investing is best for those who have experience in website development and profitable website design.

www.ingramcontent.com/pod-product-compliance
Lightning Source LLC
Chambersburg PA
CBHW060852220526
45466CB00003B/1335